Yale Studies in English
Benjamin Christie Nangle, Editor
Volume 164

Entertainment at an Elizabethan wedding feast

A detail from the portrait of Sir Henry Unton,
Elizabeth's Ambassador to France, depicting
various scenes in his life. Courtesy of the
National Portrait Gallery, London.

OMETHING OF GREAT CONSTANCY

THE ART OF "A MIDSUMMER NIGHT'S DREAM"

BY DAVID P. YOUNG

NEW HAVEN & LONDON, YALE UNIVERSITY PRESS, 1966

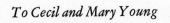

To Cecil and Mary Young

The.　*Such tricks hath strong imagination*
That, if it would but apprehend some joy,
It comprehends some bringer of that joy;
Or in the night, imagining some fear,
How easy is a bush suppos'd a bear!

Hip.　*But all the story of the night told over,*
And all their minds transfigur'd so together,
More witnesseth than fancy's images
And grows to something of great constancy;
But howsoever, strange and admirable.

Acknowledgments

This book is based closely upon a dissertation submitted to the Department of English at Yale University in the spring of 1965. It had its beginnings in materials explored in a course with Charles T. Prouty in 1960–61. Its final form owes most to the support and counsel of my adviser, Maynard Mack. His patience, wisdom, and unremitting high standards have earned a gratitude which I could not begin to express or calculate.

Chloe Hamilton Young, my wife, has provided sympathetic interest and encouragement from start to finish, as well as crucial help with the preparation of the manuscript. Newell Ellison, Jr., until his death in the summer of 1963, brought his friendship and keen critical sense to the aid of my early struggles. Robert Pierce, my colleague at Oberlin, read the manuscript at a late stage and offered generous encouragement and helpful commentary.

The book was written at Oberlin and has benefited from the support and good faith of many friends, colleagues, and students. To all of them I offer warmest and sincerest thanks.

D.P.Y.

Oberlin
April 1966

Contents

A Note on Citations

All quotations and line numberings from *A Midsummer Night's Dream* are taken from the Kittredge Edition of the play (ed. George Lyman Kittredge [Boston, Ginn and Co., 1939]). Other editions consulted include the New Variorum Edition (ed. Furness [Philadelphia, J. B. Lippincott Co., 1895]), the Temple Edition (ed. Gollancz [London, J. M. Dent, 1904]), the Arden Edition (ed. Chambers [Boston, D. C. Heath, 1909]), the Tudor Edition (ed. Cunliffe [New York, Macmillan Co., 1912]), the Yale Edition (ed. Durham [New Haven, Yale University Press, 1918]), the New Cambridge Edition (eds. J. Dover Wilson and Sir Arthur Quiller-Couch [London, Cambridge University Press, 1924]), and the New Clarendon Edition (ed. Horwood [Oxford, Clarendon Press, 1951]). Quotations from other plays by Shakespeare are taken from *The Complete Works of Shakespeare,* ed. George Lyman Kittredge (Boston, Ginn and Co., 1936).

Prologue

WORK OF CRITICISM THAT EXCEEDS ITS subject in length is rightly regarded with suspicion. Even in the arena of Shakespeare studies, where extended commentary is thought to have its virtues, the question deserves raising. A book-length analysis of *Hamlet* may pass without notice. Similar privileges can be claimed for *Lear, Macbeth,* and *Othello*. But a long work on a single comedy, especially an early comedy, is bound to arouse skepticism. Why not two comedies, or five, or ten, or all of them? I should answer that comedy ought to enjoy the same rights as tragedy and that the present study is not really very long, all things considered; but the question deserves another reply, one that touches on the problem of the appropriate subjects for our continual efforts to better understand and interpret Shakespeare's plays.

The purpose of this study of a single play is to provide an extensive, though by no means exhaustive, analysis, one that synthesizes my own findings with the work of other commentators. Many books about Shakespeare are what we might call "horizontal" in method; they take one or more aspects, themes, or devices and examine them in terms of a large group of plays, sometimes the whole canon. It is my hope that a "vertical" study of one play, combining the insights of many "horizontal" works with some new materials, will be a fresh and useful presentation. This is not to say that I wish to abjure the larger benefits of multi-play analyses, or that I intend to make no reference to earlier and later plays by Shakespeare. On the contrary, my intention is to establish the importance of *A Midsummer Night's Dream* in the development of Shakespeare's art, to redefine its place in the canon, and to emphasize its significance as a source of our knowledge of Shakespeare's own attitude toward drama, poetry, and the imagination. This end, I believe, is best achieved by a detailed study of the play rather than by extensive comparison with other plays. I shall begin and end, however, with some general remarks about the play in the perspective of its relation to Shakespeare's other works. Hopefully, the intervening study will serve to make the second look somewhat more illuminating than the first.

A Midsummer Night's Dream belongs to the group of plays mentioned by Francis Meres in 1598. Scholars generally place it eleventh or twelfth in the chronological ordering of the canon and fifth among the comedies. It is usually dated between 1594 and 1596, with 1595 the most favored year; exact dating seems nearly impossible, however, based as it is upon a few tenuous topical allusions and speculation about the occasion of the first performance. J. Dover Wilson, who has advanced a rather finespun theory of revision, thinks the play was written in 1592 and then revised in 1594 and again in 1598.[1]

The three surviving texts of the play offer no serious difficulties; they are the Fisher quarto of 1600, the "Roberts" (Jaggard) quarto of 1619 (falsely dated 1600), and the Folio text. Each text appears to be based upon the previous one, and all are quite good by Elizabethan standards.[2]

The circumstances that occasioned *A Midsummer Night's Dream* are unusual, if not unique, among Shakespeare's plays. The play appears to have been written and first performed, at

1. Discussed in the New Cambridge Edition of the play and in John Dover Wilson, *Shakespeare's Happy Comedies* (London, 1962), pp. 184 ff.

2. This is the standard view. For a slight variation, cf. Hardin Craig, *A New Look At Shakespeare's Quartos* (Stanford, 1961), pp. 108–09.

least in the version in which it survives, for a marriage celebration either in a great country house or at court. Thus, it had
a private and courtly audience as well as the public ones mentioned on the title page of the first quarto. Like a masque or
a pageant, it was designed for a particular occasion; unlike
such performances, it was not limited to the occasion. It has
enjoyed a steady popularity on the stage, with the customary
depredations of adaptors, producers, directors, and actors, up to
the present. Even those speeches in which scholars claim to find
puzzling allusions to court matters are perfectly clear in terms
of plot and on the level of normal performance. The play's
apparent duality of purpose is one of its most remarkable
features.

One of the reasons for dating *A Midsummer Night's Dream*
three or four years before the terminus a quo provided by Meres
is the evidence of earliness in its style and structure. The poetry
is often distinctly lyrical, i.e. elaborated beyond the dramatic
requirements of a given situation. There is abundant formality
of style—stichomythia, end-stopped lines, couplets, and syn-
tactical repetition. The plot is shaped with considerable emphasis on symmetry, and several of the major events are presented
with a sense of ceremony and ritual. While not all of these
features are limited to Shakespeare's early manner, they provide,
taken together, sufficient evidence to suppose that the *Dream*
predates *The Merchant of Venice* and the *Henry IV* plays.

In fact, *A Midsummer Night's Dream* is very often placed
last in the grouping of Shakespeare's early plays as an example,
along with *Romeo and Juliet* and *Richard II,* of his greatest
success in the "formal" manner, just before his technique became relaxed, natural, and distinctly personal. In the line of his
comic development, it is often described as a successful blending
of his earlier experiments with farce in *The Comedy of Errors*
and *The Taming of the Shrew* and with romance in *The Two
Gentlemen of Verona*. The comedy with which it is most fre-

quently paired is *Love's Labour's Lost*. Both, it is said, show the strong influence of Lyly in themes, characters, and plotting. But the influence of other contemporary writers of comedy, namely Greene and Peele, has also been detected in the *Dream*, with the result that it is often described as a synthesis of the prevailing comic fashions. So successful is this blending, argues Miss Bradbrook, that "it is no longer possible to distinguish separate strands of the older kinds of plays, for Shakespeare is here creating his own."[3] C. S. Baldwin has the same view:

> *Midsummer Night's Dream* is a complete fusion, not only of style, as Tasso's *Aminta*, but also in dramatic movement. As Theseus, Puck, and Bottom, the lovers and yokels, are all conformed to the same world, so they all interact in a single sequence toward a uniting issue.[4]

The basis for admiration of the *Dream*, then, has been for many its position as Shakespeare's first completely successful comedy, perhaps his first totally successful play. The particular quality of his achievement in this case seems to have stemmed from his ability to bring a great variety of comic materials into a complete harmony, a synthesis or fusion by which he was able to make them his own. This more or less standard view of the play seems to me to raise immediately several interesting questions: By what means was the playwright able to accomplish harmony in such an inclusive gathering of previously disparate comic styles? Did the dual purpose and the dual audience have something to do with his success? To what extent was the audience aware of what the playwright was accomplishing and did their awareness play any part in the accomplishment? Since the play seems to represent a great stride forward in Shake-

3. M. E. Bradbrook, *The Growth and Structure of Elizabethan Comedy* (London, 1955), p. 75.
4. Charles Sears Baldwin, *Renaissance Literary Theory and Practice* (New York, 1939), p. 153.

speare's art, what innovations in his dramaturgy can be found to have accompanied his achievement? Finally, may not the play, since it contains an inner play and discussions of drama, poetry, and the imagination, represent a very conscious effort on the part of the dramatist to advance the scope and level of his art and thus be a vital source for our understanding of Shakespeare's own ideas about the character and purpose of his art?

Some of these questions, as I shall indicate, have been partially answered by recent criticism of the *Dream*. I do not pretend to offer a revolutionary interpretation of the play. What I do claim to provide is a more thorough examination than it has had to date. Admiration for *A Midsummer Night's Dream*, while widespread, has been glancing, often characterized by a positive reluctance to scrutinize the play closely lest its charm vanish like its fairies and its moonlight. This study rests on a firm faith in the value of analysis and the durability of fairies, moonlight, and Shakespearean comedy.

Moreover, it should be pointed out that insofar as we are able to answer the questions posed above, we shall provide ourselves not only with a more thorough understanding of the excellence of the *Dream*, but with insight into Shakespeare's use of his source materials, his relationship with his audience, the means by which he was able to transcend the limitations of Elizabethan theater and turn its conditions to enormous advantage, and his own attitudes toward his achievement. Surely such matters are worth consideration, even when success must be partial, and surely it is possible that a careful analysis of a single key work may tell us as much about a dramatist as studies of groups of plays that must inevitably touch lightly on the individual work. That, at any rate, is the reasoning behind this approach.

The inquiry has been divided into three sections. The first examines the dramatic and nondramatic backgrounds of the play with emphasis on Shakespeare's manipulation of audience response to accomplish particular dramatic ends. The second takes up stylistic and structural achievements that made possible the wedding of such diverse comic materials. The third offers, through an exploration of the play's thematic preoccupations, some suggestions about the nature of Shakespeare's art and his own attitudes toward it. It is my hope that the three, taken together, will serve to justify and enrich the claim of the title, a claim that is taken from Hippolyta's astute comment on the lovers' night in the woods:

> But all the story of the night told over,
> And all their minds transfigur'd so together,
> More witnesseth than fancy's images
> And grows to something of great constancy;
> But howsoever, strange and admirable.
>
> (V.1.23–27)

1 ❋ Backgrounds

A popular audience, uncontaminated by abstract and tendentious dramatic theory, will attend to several diverse aspects of a situation, simultaneously yet without confusion. That the playwright should avail himself of this fact is a prerequisite of all dramatic subtlety. Conditions in the Elizabethan theater were ideal. . . . Such an atmosphere would favor spontaneous development. Conventions would exist, not as a conscious systematization of the playwright, but as an unconscious and organic outgrowth of playhouse psychology; a body of traditional assumptions held in common by playwright and audience.

S. L. BETHELL

THE QUESTION OF SOURCE MATERIALS and their relevance to our understanding of Shakespeare can best be examined, I think, through an example, and I have chosen that moment in the third act of *A Midsummer Night's Dream* when Titania wakens to fall in love with Bottom. The actor–weaver, deserted by his friends and unaware that he has the head of an ass, is demonstrating his bravery:

> I will walk up and down here, and will sing, that they shall hear I am not afraid.   (*sings*)

> > The woosel cock so black of hue,
> > > With orange-tawny bill,
> > The throstle with his note so true,
> > > The wren with little quill—

Tita. What angel wakes me from my flow'ry bed?

Bot. The finch, the sparrow, and the lark,
> The plain-song cuckoo gray,
Whose note full many a man doth mark,
> And dare not answer nay.

For, indeed, who would set his wit to so foolish a bird? Who would give a bird the lie, though he cry 'cuckoo' never so?

Tita. I pray thee, gentle mortal, sing again.
Mine ear is much enamoured of thy note;
So is mine eye enthralled to thy shape;

And thy fair virtue's force (perforce) doth move me,
On the first view, to say, to swear, I love thee.

Bot. Methinks, mistress, you should have little reason for that.
                                                                    (III.1.126–46)

It is a very funny moment, and a rich one. Part of its richness, as
various studies have shown, lies in its relation to a multitude of
possible sources.[1] Bottom's transformation has literary affinities
with Ovid and Apuleius and the comedies of John Lyly, as well
as with folktales of magic and witchcraft that have come down
to us through writers like Reginald Scot. Titania, as the fairy
queen, evokes a double strain of mythology and folklore, along
with the names of Chaucer and Spenser; as a goddess in love
with a mortal she recalls similar moments in Ovid and in such
Ovidian works as Shakespeare's own *Venus and Adonis* and
Lyly's comedy, *Endymion.*

Those are the precedents suggested by the outlines of the
event. The language of the passage, as is often true with
Shakespeare, invites greater particularity in the tracing of
sources. The song Bottom sings resembles a song in *The Arbor
of Amorous Devices* attributed to Richard Edwards;[2] Titania's
waking line is very reminiscent of the famous moment in *The
Spanish Tragedy* when Hieronimo stumbles on stage, awakened
by the cries of Bel-Imperia, with a speech that begins:

What outcries pluck me from my naked bed?[3]

1. Source studies of the play include Frank Sidgwick, *Sources and
Analogues of A Midsummer Night's Dream* (London, 1908); Geoffrey
Bullough, *Narrative and Dramatic Sources of Shakespeare, 1* (6 vols.
London, 1957); Kenneth Muir, *Shakespeare's Sources* (London, 1957);
and T. W. Baldwin, *The Literary Genetics of Shakespeare's Plays*
(Urbana, Ill., 1959).

2. Suggested by Hyder Edward Rollins, ed., *The Arbor of Amorous
Devices* (Cambridge, Mass., 1936), pp. xv–xvi.

3. This parallel is cited by A. P. Rossiter in his *English Drama
From Early Times to the Elizabethans* (London, 1950), p. 9.

What are we to make of this material lying beneath and behind the dramatic moment like so much carpet and tapestry? We might begin by observing that it seems unlikely that all the mentioned possibilities could be called sources, and equally unlikely that none of them are sources. But our obligation, if we are interested in the background of the dramatic event, is to consider every possibility. If we insist on accepting Lyly and dismissing Apuleius (a frequent stratagem), we are probably guilty of too much confidence in our knowledge of the playwright's education and associations or the contents of his library and his head. Better to assume that most of the richness is there and that it deserves attention.

When we have determined, more or less, what the sources are, our next occupation must be to discover why they are there, what use the dramatist has put them to. For this effort we must think of them in terms of their calculated effect on the audience. It is of very little interest simply to know, as from a list, what books Shakespeare had read and what plays he had seen, but it is of great interest to discover what use he was able to put them to in his art. The condition of drama, after all, is in the expectations and reactions of the audience. No one knows better than the dramatist that the realization of everything he aims at must occur in the response of a large and diverse body of spectators. That is why successful drama is always a combination of the familiar and the novel or surprising. The former is necessary for any common response from a group of people; the latter, for their interest and entertainment as well as the playwright's uniqueness, his point of view.

The sources of a drama, then, often belong under the heading of the familiar, the shared experiences from which the playwright creates the circumstances and atmosphere of his play. We know this to be true when we witness or read a Greek tragedy based on a familiar myth and, often, on other plays. Perhaps we sense it when we see Falstaff, who combines familiar types

—the braggart soldier, the morality Vice, the jester, the tricky servant—in a way that is entirely unique.[4] But the fact is that we often forget the principle in studies of Shakespeare's sources. We note the familiar elements, but not the use to which they have been put or the way in which they interact with what is new. As long as such failures attend the study of sources, the devastating question, "So what?" remains to plague them.

If we return now to the original example, Bottom confronting Titania, we find that Shakespeare's use of the familiar offers a very mixed bag. There are few sources that could have been familiar to every member of· the audience. The play was probably commissioned as part of a wedding celebration and played first before a courtly audience,[5] but it was also seen on the public stage, so that it reached, finally, a cross section of Elizabethan society. The familiar elements in this moment of confrontation seem to reach out to the full range of the cross section. A reasonably literate man would have seen in Bottom's transformation the parallels in the stories of Midas, Circe, and Apuleius. Less-educated members of the audience would rely on folklore stories of human–animal metamorphosis for their recognition. Only an inveterate playgoer, one would think, could have caught the reference to *The Spanish Tragedy* (I am convinced it is one), although his amusement was likely to be boisterous. Many would know the fairies and their queen from masques and pageants, but they had also been seen in the theaters recently in the plays of Lyly and Greene. Even a man who had never been to a play before (unlikely Elizabethan!)

4. Cf. Northrop Frye, "Characterization in Shakespearean Comedy," *Shakespeare Quarterly*, 4 (1953), 271 ff.

5. Commentators find it hard to agree on which wedding the play was commissioned for. For discussion of possibilities, see E. K. Chambers, *William Shakespeare* (2 vols. Oxford, 1930), *1*, pp. 358–59, and Wilson, *Shakespeare's Happy Comedies*, pp. 192 ff. The dissenter to the wedding theory is Baldwin, *Literary Genetics*, p. 480. His remarks are not convincing.

would recognize a connection between Bottom and the animal-headed figures of mumming and morris-dancing and gain some orientation from that. In short, there is enough of the familiar in this strange and hilarious moment to arouse every sort of recognition and to weld a disparate audience into a manageable unit of response.

What is especially interesting about the meeting of Bottom and Titania, however, is the quality of its unfamiliarity, rising from the conjunction of familiar elements. Most of the audience, we can assume, could recognize the two figures—Bottom as clown, ass, and mummer, Titania as literary symbol and masque heroine—drawn from separate worlds. What is novel is the experience of seeing them together on the same stage. From that juxtaposition rises the humor of the moment and its meaning for the audience. As Bottom meets Titania, analogies begin to surround them: the popular stage joins hands with the world of court entertainment; folklore is introduced to myth; grossness chats with refinement; bestiality dallies with spirituality. The meanings are wordless and rapid; they require no other articulation than the dramatic moment itself. But they are based, necessarily, on the associations already held by the audience with the two separate figures and their separate worlds and on the dramatist's ability to bring them together effectively. The evidence of such skillful blending on Shakespeare's part confirms the frequent assertions that *A Midsummer Night's Dream* is a remarkable synthesis of comic materials, a courtly comedy with enough appeal for the popular stage.

The question for this chapter, then, is not so much which sources Shakespeare used in the play—that has been determined elsewhere—as why he used them and what their theatrical effect was. Some of the answers must wait for later chapters, but this first one will rapidly survey the diverse elements of the play and their immediate uses. I shall try to keep the discussion open for the full spectrum of reaction in the audience. If there were only one man in England astute enough to catch the line from Kyd, that man and that line and their interaction would merit attention. We must grant the dramatist the same privileges we grant the novelist and the poet—an ideal auditor, reader, or spectator. Our primary attention, nevertheless, must be to the difficult question of the response of the audience as a group to the effective manipulations of the dramatist.

THE NONDRAMATIC BACKGROUND

"With pomp, with triumph, and with revelling"   Shakespeare created an ambience of festivity for *A Midsummer Night's Dream* by associating it with three kinds of celebration—royal marriage and the May and Midsummer holidays. The first of these is established at the very outset with the introduction of the event that frames the action—a famous wedding from antiquity. Theseus clearly sees his marriage as the occasion for a national fete; he is no sooner on stage than he begins to issue instructions for communal celebration:

> Go, Philostrate,
> Stir up the Athenian youth to merriments,
> Awake the pert and nimble spirit of mirth,
> Turn melancholy forth to funerals;
> The pale companion is not for our pomp.
>
> (I.1.11–15)

He turns to his bride with an explanation:

> Hippolyta, I woo'd thee with my sword,
> And won thy love, doing thee injuries;
> But I will wed thee in another key,
> With pomp, with triumph, and with revelling.
>
> (I.1.16–19)

Shakespeare adapted this aspect of Theseus' character from Plutarch and Chaucer. Plutarch presents a Theseus who is, among other things, founder of a city and establisher of communal feasts and games, the inventor, in a sense, of holiday.[6] Chaucer's character is a wise and pleasure-loving ruler who is married with "muchel glorie and greet solempnytee"[7] and who, when trouble arrives, usually seeks to resolve it through some kind of ceremony. Thus, he makes a magnificent tournament out of the quarrel between Palamon and Arcite. After the accident that befalls Arcite, he decides to go ahead with the festival:

> And made revel al the longe nyght
> Unto the straunge lordes, as was right
>
> . . .
>
> And yaf hem yiftes after hir degree,
> And fully heeld a feeste dayes three.[8]

Upon Arcite's death, he arranges a magnificent funeral. When the mourning has subsided, he calls a parliament and, after an eloquent speech in which he sets forth his view of change and mortality as part of the natural harmony, proposes that Emelye and Palamon marry. They are wed with "alle blisse and melodye."

Shakespeare's Duke Theseus is very close in behavior and ideals to these sources. While the portrait of him as sponsor of festivals and patron of the arts may have been a glancing compliment to whichever nobleman originally commissioned the *Dream,* he is clearly essential to Shakespeare in setting the tone of the comedy. Whatever discords arise promise to be resolved

6. The relevant passages from North's *Plutarch* are in Bullough, *Narrative and Dramatic Sources,* pp. 384–89.

7. *The Knighte's Tale,* in Geoffrey Chaucer, *Works,* ed. F. N. Robinson (Boston, 1957), p. 25 (870).

8. Ibid., p. 43 (2717–18, 2735–36).

in the accommodating and joyous atmosphere of the royal wedding.[9]

Not content, however, to rely simply upon the mood of marriage for his comic synthesis, the playwright broadens and extends the sense of festival by linking the action to two holidays familiar to every member of the audience—May Day, more particularly the custom of "Maying," and Midsummer Eve. Each has a special significance.

Chaucer's mention of May customs in *The Knighte's Tale* may have suggested the connection to Shakespeare. Palamon and Arcite first see Emelye gathering flowers on a May morning:

> For May wole have no slogardie a-nyght.
> The sesoun priketh every gentil herte,
> And maketh hym out of his sleep to sterte,
> And seith, "arys, and do thyn observaunce."
> This maked Emelye have remembraunce
> To doon honour to May, and for to ryse.[10]

Later in the story, Arcite rides to the wood "for to doon his observaunce to May," behaving, Chaucer tells us, very much like any other love-struck youth. Hence, Chaucer attaches his themes of love and ritual to a particular holiday custom, the gathering of hawthorn branches early in May.

The connection, however, was not merely Chaucer's; it was present in the holiday itself. No literacy was required for an audience to understand that the "rite of May" was both an individual and a communal means of celebrating the arrival of spring and reestablishing the human affinity with the natural cycles. As C. L. Barber describes it:

9. For a fuller discussion of the marriage ideal, see Paul A. Olson, "*A Midsummer Night's Dream* and the Meaning of Court Marriage," *ELH*, 24 (1957), 95–119.
10. Chaucer, *Works*, p. 27 (1042–47).

The bringing home of May acted out an experience of the relationship between vitality in people and nature. The poets have merely to describe May Day to develop a metaphor relating man and nature.[11]

As the phrase "acted out" indicates, we have in the holiday a potential dramatic situation as well as a metaphor. The ritual movement to the woods performed by lover and community is reflected in the very structure of Shakespeare's play, and the connection is enforced by specific references. Lysander arranges to meet the eloping Hermia,

> in the wood, a league without the town
> Where I did meet thee once with Helena
> To do observaunce to a morn of May,
> There will I stay for thee.
>
> (I.1.165–68)

Helena mentions "hawthorn buds" (i.e. May) shortly after (line 185), and the mechanicals, when they rehearse in the woods, choose a hawthorn brake as their tiring house (III.1.5). This brake is the scene of Bottom's offstage transformation. In the fourth act, when the hunting party stumbles upon the sleeping lovers, Theseus charitably observes:

> No doubt they rose up early to observe
> The rite of May; and, hearing our intent,
> Came here in grace of our solemnity.
>
> (IV.1.135–37)

Theseus himself thus links marriage and Maying. A moment later he mentions still another holiday, emphasizing the license

11. C. L. Barber, *Shakespeare's Festive Comedy* (Princeton, 1959), pp. 18–19. I am in debt to Prof. Barber's excellent account of the relation between English holidays and social customs, and Shakespearean comedy.

associated with festivity and its connection with natural fertility:

> Good morrow, friends. Saint Valentine is past.
> Begin these woodbirds but to couple now?
>
> (IV.1.142–43)

It is not surprising that such holiday customs were under attack from the puritans.[12] For most of Shakespeare's audience, however, the associations were pleasant and their meaning clear.

Midsummer Eve, associated with the summer solstice, is one of the oldest and most widely celebrated holidays on record. Originally intended as homage to the sun at the height of his powers, it had become by Shakespeare's time a night of general merriment with overtones of magic. Its customary features included the building of bonfires and the carrying of torches, the gathering of plants with magical and medicinal virtues, rituals intended for love divinations, and all-night watches. More generally, it was thought to be a time when spirits were abroad and strange events occurred. All of these aspects were absorbed into Shakespeare's comedy.

The direct reference to the holiday is in the title, where it conceivably acts upon the expectations of the audience before the play begins. An Elizabethan audience would have been led to expect several things from a play about Midsummer Eve. First, there would be scenes in the woods, for that was where one went to gather, by moonlight and at midnight, the special plants that might bring one luck, make one invisible, or reveal one's love—orpine, fern seed, Saint-John's-wort. Next, it would come as no surprise that there were spirits in the woods, spirits capable of playing tricks on those who entered their domain:

> Fern-seed . . . must be gathered on Midsummer Eve. A person who went to gather it reported that the Spirits whisked by

12. E.g. the well-known passage in Phillip Stubbes, *The Anatomy of Abuses,* ed. F. J. Furnivall (London, 1877), p. 149. Cited in Barber, p. 21.

his ears, and sometimes struck his hat and other parts of his body, and at length, when he thought he had a good quantity of it, and secured it in papers and a box, when he came home, he found both empty.[13]

Illusions were common in the woods. One such was fool's fire, ignis fatuus, seen around churchyards, rivers, and swamps. A traveler following such a light was apt to end up in a bog or a mire, and popular tradition held that the light was a spirit deliberately leading night wanderers astray. While this phenomenon was not limited to Midsummer Eve, it must have had a special significance at that time, as it would inevitably be connected with the blooming of the oak, the fern, and the mistletoe, consecrated plants reputed to bloom and glow only on Midsummer Eve.[14] The spirit responsible for fool's fire had several names, among them Robin Goodfellow. A contemporary ballad enumerating his disguises adds:

> Sometime he'd counterfeit a voyce,
>   and travellers call astray.
> Sometimes a walking fire he'd be
>   and lead them from their way.
>
> Some call him Robin Good-fellow,
>   Hob-goblin or mad Crisp,
> And some againe doe tearme him oft,
>   by name of Will the Wispe.[15]

Thus, Puck arrives naturally in the play through the Midsummer

13. W. Carew Hazlitt, ed., *Brand's Popular Antiquities of Great Britain* (3 vols. London, 1870), *1, 179.*

14. See in J. G. Frazer, "The Solar Theory of Fire Festivals," *The Golden Bough* (abridged ed. London, 1954), pp. 643 ff. The oak is mentioned in the play. The mechanicals are to meet in the woods for their rehearsal "at the Duke's oak" (I.2.97).

15. J. O. Halliwell-Phillips, *Illustrations of the Fairy Mythology of A Midsummer Night's Dream* (London, 1845), p. 164.

entrance; we have no sooner seen him than we hear him described as one who will:

> Mislead night-wanderers, laughing at their harm.
>
> (II.1.39)

The whole night of error in the woods, with Goodfellow as
chief prankster, apparently derived its familiar qualities from
the Midsummer holiday and the accompanying notion of "midsummer madness."

Not all fires to be seen on Midsummer Eve were illusory.
The man-made fires were called "blessing fires." Leaping
through them or dancing round them was supposed to insure
fertility, innocence, good luck, and easy childbirth.[16] Torches
kindled at these fires were carried in processions and used to
light hearthfires. These associations are gathered in at the end
of *A Midsummer Night's Dream* when the fairies reenter to
bless the marriage. Oberon's first instructions to his troop are:

> Through the house give glimmering light
> By the dead and drowsy fire;
>
> (V.1.398–99)

Presumably the fairies kindle their torches at the hearthfire and
dance with them. Titania then orders them to perform the ritual
blessing:

> Hand in hand with fairy grace,
> Will we sing and bless this place.
>
> (V.1.406–07)

Shakespeare here performs a reversal. Such blessings were usually intended to keep fairies and other spirits away, since it was
thought that they might interfere in matters of fertility and
childbearing, perhaps even steal children for their own use.

16. See Hazlitt, *Brand's Antiquities*, pp. 169 ff., and Frazer, *Golden
Bough*, pp. 643 ff.

That they perform the purification themselves emphasizes their ultimate benevolence.

The association of Midsummer with marriage was probably quite natural to Shakespeare's audience. June is traditionally the marriage month, and in some European countries Midsummer Eve is still a time for both actual and ceremonial marriages, with the choosing of a "Midsummer's Bride" who in turn selects a bridegroom.[17] Further evidence for the association can be found in Spenser's *Epithalamion.* Spenser was married on St. Barnabas Day, June 11, the time of the actual solstice by the old calendar,[18] but in exploring the significance of the date he draws upon the customs of the Midsummer holiday:

> Ring ye the bels, to make it weare away,
> And bonefiers make all day,
> And daunce about them, and about them sing:
> That all the woods may answer, and your eccho ring.[19]

When night arrives, the poet's benediction again reminds us of elements of the *Dream:*

> Let no deluding dreames, nor dreadful sights
> Make sudden sad affrights;
> Ne let housefyres, nor lightnings helpelesse harmes,
> Ne let the Pouke, nor other evill sprights,
> Ne let mischivous witches with theyr charmes,
> Ne let hob Goblins, names whose sense we see not,
> Fray us with things that be not.[20]

17. Frazer, p. 132.

18. Cf. the very thorough analysis of this poem by A. Kent Hieatt, *Short Time's Endless Monument* (New York, 1960).

19. Edmund Spenser, *Works,* Cambridge Edition, ed. R. E. Neil Dodge (Boston, 1908), p. 738.

20. Ibid., p. 739.

Spenser sounds a little like Theseus here; he does not quite share Shakespeare's comic and affirmative attitude toward dreams and "the Pouke," but both poets pick up the same details, presumably because they were already associated with the holiday, as the holiday, in turn, was associated with marriage.

Commentators have experienced difficulty with Shakespeare's use of two separate holidays in one play; this use, together with the references to the moon in its various stages, has engendered much discussion about the time scheme. The temptation is usually to emphasize one holiday at the expense of the other (e.g. Bullough's recent assertion that "The action takes place on the night before May-day").[21] The custom of Maying, however, as Barber has pointed out, was not confined to May Day.[22] Similarly, "midsummer madness" can descend upon its victims at times other than the night of June 23.[23] In both cases, Shakespeare is interested in making use of the associations aroused by his mention of the two holidays rather than in dating the action of his play. In fact, it seems clear that he has deliberately created a blurring of time in the play in order to dismiss calendar time and establish a more elusive festival time. Marriage gives the story its proper comic framework and sense of order. May Day introduces the theme of infatuated love and, taking the play to the woods, sets up the metaphor relating man and nature. Midsummer Eve, still in the woods, turns day to night and extends the natural so as to accommodate madness, mystery, and the supernatural in the form of the spirits, thus broadening the implications of the metaphor. The ambience of festivity is complex and resonant, and it depends for its effectiveness upon the audience's recognition and assent.

21. Bullough, *Narrative and Dramatic Sources,* p. 367.
22. Barber, *Shakespeare's Festive Comedy,* p. 120.
23. Cf. *Twelfth Night,* III.4.61. A few lines later we have, "More matter for a May morning." Apparently Shakespeare had not gotten over his "confusion" about the two holidays.

The Myth on the Churchway Path   Most of the folklore in *A Midsummer Night's Dream* can be associated with the holidays, as in the cases of Goodfellow and Midsummer Eve, but it also deserves to be discussed in connection with mythology, because the playwright, as if pursuing an analogy between the two, constantly combines myth and folktale in a way that was new to the drama.

The references to the moon provide a good example of this interaction. The moon that shines in the Athenian woods is of course a classical moon, associated with Phoebe (I.1.209) and the triple goddess, Hecate-Diana-Proserpina (V.1.391), at once chaste and wanton, a symbol of change and transmutation. But it is also a homely English moon, a moon of "moonshine" in which one can discern a man with a thornbush and a dog. The two moons fit together nicely because their aspects are so much alike. Both are "the governess of floods" (II.1.103) and sponsor of lunacy. Phoebe, "decking with liquid pearl the bladed grass" (I.1.211), is the same mysterious presence under whose crescent a farmer might plant his beans to insure their fertility or a young girl curtsey and ask for a good dream:

> New Moon, new Moon, I hail thee;
> By all the virtue in thy body,
> Grant that this night I may see
> Him who my true love is to be.[24]

Thus, myth and folklore readily complement each other; the former invokes the learning and literature of antiquity, the myths that were supposed to contain secrets of nature, while the latter calls up for the audience the more immediate, and perhaps less respectable, wisdom of the country, the charms and spirits that were used to explain and propitiate nature's mysterious power over man's life and behavior. That the two were

24. Cited in Eleanor Hull, *Folklore of the British Isles* (London, 1928), p. 64.

essentially the same was by no means evident to the Elizabethans. Writers like Bacon and Burton had great respect for myths and almost none for what they called superstitions and bugbears. The term "folklore," however, suggests barriers that did not exist for the average Elizabethan. If he could doubt the existence of such mysteries, he could as easily see them as part of the fabric of life.

What is true of the moon applies to the fairies. They are a curious mixture of wood spirits and household gods, pagan deities and local pixies. They inhabit the environs of Athens and follow the fortunes of Theseus and Hippolyta, but they are clearly the spirits whom we can consider "almost essential to a Midsummer Play,"[25] detectably English in character and habit. Through Titania and her train, Shakespeare emphasizes their innocence and delicacy; in Oberon and Puck, he expresses their darker side, potentially malevolent in the lore of the time.

The mixture of qualities is pointed up in their language. Oberon, who is named from a popular French romance, *Huon of Bordeaux,* and Titania, whose name is Ovidian, continually refer to myths that are parts of their own lives:

> Why art thou here,
> Come from the farthest steep of India,
> But that, forsooth, the bouncing Amazon,
> Your buskin'd mistress and your warrior love,
> To Theseus must be wedded . . . ?

> *Ober.*   How canst thou thus, for shame, Titania,
> Glance at my credit with Hippolyta,
> Knowing I know thy love for Theseus?

25. Bullough, *Narrative and Dramatic Sources,* p. 370. It is not easy to tell just *how* essential. Much of the corroborative evidence is not directly from English folklore. See, for example, the information about Aine of Knockainy, the Irish "fairy queen," cited in Hull, *Folklore,* pp. 50–51.

> Didst thou not lead him through the glimmering night
> From Perigouna, whom he ravished?
> And make him with fair Ægles break his faith,
> With Ariadne, and Antiopa?
>
> (II.1.68–80)

This side of the fairies aligns them with the fashions in court poetry, masque, and drama. To it, however, Shakespeare adds a native strain that brings them into more familiar surroundings. The flower that is responsible for the changes in the woods is "Cupid's flower," but it is also "love-in-idleness," the familiar pansy. Titania may have a classical heritage, but her companions are named Cobweb, Peaseblossom, and Mustardseed, diminutive creatures with no flavor of antiquity.

It is Robin Goodfellow, the English national prankster, who is responsible for the greatest dose of folklore in the play. His activities, described soon after his entrance, have nothing to do with the world of myth; they belong to the barnyard, the dairy, and the local grove. His language is studded not with names from Ovid but with country proverbs:

> Jack shall have Jill;
> Naught shall go ill;
> The man shall have his mare again, and all shall be well.
>
> (III.2.461–63)

Minor White Latham, who thinks there was no precedent for Goodfellow's presence among the fairies, says of its effect:

> Though the presentation of Robin Goodfellow as a member of the fairy race may have gone counter to the accepted canons of folk belief, Shakespeare's introduction of him among his fairies . . . gave evidence both of his knowledge of folklore and of his genius. Of all the spirits who were believed to haunt England, there was not one whom he could have better chosen to give a sense of reality to his fairy plot,

or to furnish, to an audience, the immediate assurance of
boisterous gayety and of harmless fun.[26]

I must take exception to "harmless." The creature variously
called puck, pouka, pixie, bugbear, and hobgoblin, as well as the
other fairies, was dangerous, and an Elizabethan audience could
not contemplate him or his associates as representatives of the
unknown without some apprehension. Reginald Scot speaks
for all those whose mothers

> have so fraied us with bull-beggers, spirits, witches, urchens,
> elves, hags, fairies, satyrs, pans, faunes, sylens, kit with
> the cansticke, tritons, centaures, dwarfes, giants, imps, calcars,
> conjurors, nymphes, changelings, Incubus, Robin Good fel-
> low, the spoorn, the mare, the man in the oke, the hellwaine,
> the firedrake, the puckle, Tom thombe, hobgoblin, Tom
> tumbler boneles, and such other bugs, that we are afraid of
> our own shadows.[27]

As a result, he continues, even "a right hardie man" has difficulty making himself pass a churchyard at night and keeping
his hair from standing on end.

Fairies were sometimes said to be fallen angels and inhabi-
tants of hell, so that a certain confusion about their moral status
probably existed among the audience.[28] This is evident from
the pains Shakespeare takes to clear up the matter:

> *Puck.*   My fairy lord, this must be done with haste,
> For night's swift dragons cut the clouds full fast,
> And yonder shines Aurora's harbinger;

26. Minor White Latham, *The Elizabethan Fairies* (New York,
1930), p. 221.

27. Reginald Scot, *The Discoverie of Witchcraft* (London, 1930),
p. 86. Also in Bullough, *Narrative and Dramatic Sources,* p. 396. Note
that Scot's list contains some classical monsters, one precedent for
Shakespeare's mixing of myth and folklore.

28. Latham's discussion in *Elizabethan Fairies* makes this clear.

At whose approach ghosts, wand'ring here and there,
Troop home to churchyards; damned spirits all,
That in crossways and floods have burial,
Already to their wormy beds are gone.
For fear lest day should look their shames upon,
They willfully themselves exile from light,
And must for aye consort with black-brow'd night.

Ober.   But we are spirits of another sort.
I with the morning's love have oft made sport;
And, like a forester, the groves may tread
Even till the eastern gate, all fiery red,
Opening on Neptune, with fair blessed beams
Turns into yellow gold his salt green streams.

(III.2.378–93)

Here is another mixture of the local and the classical, the one
used to resolve the other. Robin's apprehension is not in fact
very plausible; he must know already what Oberon so eloquently
tells him. Shakespeare apparently thought the exchange a necessary piece of exposition, a firm reminder to his audience that his
fairies were not demons.

Modern productions, overstressing the nondemonic, have
seriously misrepresented the fairies as gauzy, fluttery creatures
with no more mystery or authority than butterflies. Something is
lost by this. Oberon is not harmless; he is a prince from the
furthest steep of India, shadowy and exotic. Titania is a powerful force—"The summer still doth tend upon my state"—and
Bottom is virtually her prisoner. The marital disturbances of
these beings affect the weather and the natural cycles and result
in floods, droughts, and famines. Their benevolent presence in
this play serves to emphasize the comic context only if they are
recognized as potentially dangerous.[29]

29. W. Moelwyn Merchant, in a survey of the play's stage history
(*"A Midsummer Night's Dream:* A Visual Re-creation," *Early Shake-*

As far as the stage was concerned, few precedents of any significance existed for Shakespeare's mixture of myth and folklore. The comedies of the 1580s had successfully used both, Greene and Peele exploiting folklore and Lyly working with myth, but there had been little serious attempt to mix the two. *The Old Wives' Tale* begins with some passages that may have interested Shakespeare:

> And, in faith, sir, unless your hospitality do relieve us, we are like to wander, with a sorrowful heigh-ho, among the owlets and hobgoblins of the forest. Good Vulcan, for Cupid's sake that hath cozened us all, befriend us as thou mayst.
>
> (Ind.11.45 f.)[30]

This is the sort of texture that could be achieved by the interaction of learning and lore, but Peele does not maintain it and his play remains simply a hint of what was to come.

If there are few dramatic precedents to speak of, however, there are literary examples that deserve mention, notably in Chaucer and Spenser. What Shakespeare might have learned from the tales of the Knight and the Merchant, as well as from the *Legend of Good Women,* was that it was possible to combine distant event and local custom, the arcane and the mundane, to good effect. Maying in ancient Athens, Pluto and Proserpina

---

speare. Stratford-upon-Avon Studies 3 [New York, 1961], pp. 165–85), notes this difficulty and praises the Benjamin Britten–John Piper operatic collaboration for overcoming it. "The whole production," he notes, "had at once the frightening clarity of a nightmare and the blurred edges of a dream" (p. 182). He calls the opera version "the richest and most faithful interpretation of Shakespeare's intentions in *A Midsummer Night's Dream* that the stage has seen in our generation" (p. 183).

30. See C. F. Tucker Brooke and Nathaniel Burton Paradise, *The English Drama 1580–1642* (Boston, 1933), p. 25. Older plays like *Thersites* and *Clyomon and Clamydes* yield similar, if somewhat feebler, examples.

as king and queen of the fairies observing January and May, Alceste identified with the daisy—all were effective amalgamations. Spenser picked up the same device for *The Shepherd's Calendar* and *The Faerie Queene*. It was Shakespeare, however, who put it on the stage, and in so doing he found a means of uniting a diverse audience and refreshing mythology at the sources from which it originally sprang. It is quite true of this play that its "symbols come not from the Celtic twilight but from more conscious and intellectual literary traditions."[31] But it is also true that Shakespeare summons that twilight to give those traditions an immediacy and reality they would not otherwise have had. The combination supports some of the best moments in the play:

> Now it is the time of night
> That the graves, all gaping wide,
> Every one lets forth his sprite,
> In the churchway paths to glide;
> And we fairies, that do run
> By the triple Hecate's team
> From the presence of the sun,
> Following darkness like a dream,
> Now are frolic.
>
> (V.1.386–95)

The ideal spectator would be sophisticated enough to catch the implications of the reference to the triple Hecate and to recognize the value of the conjunction of "antique fable" and "fairy toy" (earlier condemned by Theseus), the myth on the churchway path. The less than ideal spectator would at least be provoked to remember those moments when his own hair stood on end and his eyeballs rolled in the presence of mystery.

31. Olson, *"A Midsummer Night's Dream* and the Meaning of Court Marriage," p. 118. Olson insists on dismissing folklore to make room for "intellectual literary traditions," but surely they can and do coexist.

One other feature of Elizabethan life deserves mention in any discussion of the blending of folklore and myth—the "Progresses" of Queen Elizabeth. It was the task of the Queen's host when she was visiting a country house on one of her summer Progresses to provide a more or less continuous stream of entertainment. There were masques, feasts, plays, concerts, and displays of fireworks. And there were lesser diversions. The Queen, during a tour of the grounds, might come upon small tableaux from mythology or encounter figures who claimed to be the victims of enchantments from which only someone as powerful and good as Elizabeth could release them. Such moments, with their blendings of the real and the fictive, were precious to her subjects. They gave the human activities with which she was surrounded a special status and meaning; for the moment, they had the quality of myth. But the myth, in such cases, was not distant in time and space; it grew up in a native setting, on the grounds of English country houses, with a resulting force and immediacy. It was no doubt to draw upon such associations that Shakespeare put into the mouth of Oberon a description of a royal entertainment, probably at Kenilworth or Elvetham. If the Queen were present, she presumably would have been flattered, but the wider effect, whether she was present or not, was to remind the audience of a well-known instance in which myth had the local relevance and familiarity of folklore, and folklore had the force and respectability of myth.

THE DRAMATIC BACKGROUND

Discussions of the antecedents of Shakespeare's plays usually concentrate more heavily on nondramatic sources than on earlier plays. There are at least two reasons for this. The first is practical: even though we have evidence of their existence, most of the older plays have not survived. The second is emotional: so many passionate opinions surround the theories of memorial recon-

struction and revision that it is difficult to make simple assertions about the playwright's practice. But surely, even if we
confine ourselves to the early comedies, there is a great deal
of evidence that Shakespeare was in the habit of reworking
and synthesizing material that had already been on the stage.
The Comedy of Errors is based on two of Plautus' comedies and,
very likely, on an earlier play called *The History of Error*.[32]
The Taming of the Shrew is based either on *A Shrew* or some
earlier play that the two have in common.[33] Just because we
have lost the 1585 court play of *Felix and Felismena* does not
mean that it is not a more probable source for *The Two Gentlemen of Verona* than Montemayor's romance. The fact that the
characters in the first quarto of *Love's Labour's Lost* are desig-
nated by type-names—"Pedant," "Braggart," "Clown"—suggests
that the playwright may have been revising an older play or
that he was deliberately experimenting with dramatic types;
in either case, it indicates an awareness of theatrical means and
conventions that is too little emphasized in discussions of the
influences behind Shakespeare's earlier plays.

When we turn to *A Midsummer Night's Dream* we find that
it differs from the four comedies that precede it in offering a
greater variety of dramatic materials and, consequently, a
complexity of possible sources. It is my contention that in this
play Shakespeare was trying to improve upon his own earlier
efforts and those of his predecessors. The amalgam of styles
and means indicates a conviction that the key to improvement
was inclusiveness, the wedding of elements previously considered incompatible. This successful synthesis was accomplished
with a certain degree of self-consciousness. An examination of
that self-consciousness, along with a tracing out of the comic

32. Cf. Bullough, *Narrative and Dramatic Sources*, p. 3.
33. Bullough (ibid., p. 57) holds the second view. All the information in the paragraph is drawn from Bullough and from E. K. Chambers,
The Elizabethan Stage (4 vols. Oxford, 1923).

strands that make up the play's fabric, should make this clear.
It would be well to begin where the self-consciousness is most
intense—in the handling of the mechanicals and their efforts
at court drama.

Ercles' Vein   The mechanicals, as we learn when we meet them,
are planning an "enterlude"—a short play staged in a banquet
hall—"before the Duke and Duchess, on his wedding day at
night" (I.2.6–8). We are thus prepared for an older play and
for some implicit contrasts between earlier dramaturgy and the
author's practice. Anxious to cater to royal tastes, the craftsmen
are undertaking a story from classical mythology rather than
the tale of a "wandering knight" or a "tyrant" which they would
prefer.[34] In all other respects, however, their play reflects the
worst aspects of the popular drama of the 1570s and 80s.

Their lack of sophistication is clear from Quince's working
title: "The most Lamentable Comedy and most Cruel Death of
Pyramus and Thisby." By the fifth act they have altered this
without improving it: "A tedious brief scene of young Pyramus
and his love Thisby; very tragical mirth." Shakespeare is here
having fun at the expense of the "Mungrell tragy-comedys" to
which Sidney objected, plays of the sixties and seventies in
which classical or historical subjects were crossed with moral-
ities and interludes. Most of Shakespeare's audience had probably seen and applauded plays like *Horestes* and *Cambises* on the
stage. They were now apparently ready to laugh at them. The
full title of Preston's play is "A lamentable tragedye, mixed
full of plesant mirth, containing the life of Cambises, king of
Persia."[35] Shakespeare may also have had in mind plays like

34. A glance through the Chamber and Revels Accounts in Chambers, *Elizabethan Stage, 4,* appendix B, 142 ff., will show how steadily
the fashion for subjects from antiquity had grown during the seventies
and eighties.
35. Collected in W. Carew Hazlitt, ed., *Dodsley's Old English Plays*
(15 vols. London, 1874), *4,* 157–248. See also *I Henry IV,* II.4.425:
"I must speak in passion, and I will do it in King Cambises' vein."

Appius and Virginia and *Damon and Pythias,* both of which announce themselves as "tragical comedy."[36]

The acting style associated with these plays was exaggerated, and the language was full of rhetorical effects. Bottom describes its impact:

> That will ask some tears in the true performing of it. If I do it, let the audience look to their eyes! I will move storms; I will condole in some measure. To the rest. Yet my chief humour is for a tyrant. I could play Ercles rarely, or a part to tear a cat in, to make all split.
>
> (I.2.26–32)

The posturing and ranting to which Bottom refers was going out of fashion by the 1590s. As drama replaced rhetoric on the stage, characters could be represented more naturalistically, and the thundering tyrants began to disappear. The contrast between the earlier dramatists' handling of their tyrants and Shakespeare's handling of Bottom serves a purpose beyond its unquestionable hilarity: as the drama advances to more sophisticated levels, at once subtler and more complex, the dramatist can insure that he has taken the audience with him by providing a measure of the distance between old and new, a measure that will serve to define and stabilize what has so suddenly been accomplished.

We might add that not all of the fun in the passage in question is aimed at the popular stage. Listen to Bottom's sample rant:

> The raging rocks
> And shivering shocks

36. Richard Edwards, *Damon and Pythias,* in Hazlitt, *Dodsley, 4,* 13: "Which matter mix'd with mirth and care, a just name to apply, / As seems most fit, we have it termed a tragical comedy." *Appius and Virginia* was titled: "A new Tragicall Comedie of Appius and Virginia" (Ibid., pp. 105–55).

> Shall break the locks
> Of prison gates;
> And Phibbus' car
> Shall shine from far
> And make and mar
> The foolish Fates.
> (I.2.33–40)

This is properly grandiose and meaningless, and no doubt Bottom's delivery of it recalled the Hercules whose twelve labors Robert Greene had seen terribly thundered on the popular stage;[37] but the passage itself can be linked to Jaspar Heywood's 1561 translation of Seneca's *Hercules Furens:*

> The roaring rocks have quaking stirr'd
> And none therat have push'd;
> Hell gloomy gates I have brast ope
> Where grisly ghosts all hush'd
>
> . . .
>
> O Lord of ghosts! whose fiery flash
> That forth thy hand doth shake,
> Doth cause the trembling lodges twain
> Of Phoebus car to shake.[38]

Those members of the audience who were familiar enough with Heywood's play to recognize the parody were thus served with a reference to a style that had won critical admiration. There is more than one way, apparently, "to tear a cat." Here

37. Robert Greene, *Greene's Groatsworth of Wit,* in C. M. Ingleby, ed., *Shakspere Allusion-Book* (London, 1909), p. 23.

38. Cited in the New Cambridge Edition, p. 109. Date is incorrectly given as 1581. (For correct date, see Chambers, *Elizabethan Stage, 3,* 477.) The note continues: "That there is some connexion between these lines and Bottom's looks very possible; yet there seems no reason why Shakespeare should burlesque a translation ten or a dozen years old." One wonders what sort of reason the editors require.

Shakespeare parts company with Sidney; his barbs are aimed not
so much at the unorthodox as the inept.

If the interlude is finally the utter failure that we watch in
the last act, much of the blame must be placed on its literary
style. The language of "Pyramus and Thisby" is insistently poetic
—at least in the mechanicals' terms—and for that reason it is
just as insistently undramatic. Not only is the poetry bad, but
it continually works, through its formality and artificiality, to
destroy all dramatic illusion. The rehearsal in the third act
points this up by punctuating the stilted poetry of the interlude
with the natural comments of its principals:

> *Quin.*   Speak, Pyramus. Thisby, stand forth.
> *Pyr.*   Thisby, the flowers of odious savours sweet—
> *Quin.*   Odorous! Odorous!
> *Pyr.*   —odours savours sweet;
> So hath thy breath my dearest Thisby dear.
> But hark, a voice! Stay thou but here awhile,
>   And by and by I will to thee appear.
> *Rob.*   A stranger Pyramus than e'er play'd here!
> *This.*   Must I speak now?
> *Quin.*   Ay, marry, must you; for you must understand he
> goes but to see a noise that he heard, and is to come again.
> *This.*   Most radiant Pyramus, most lily-white of hue,
>   Of colour like the red rose on triumphant brier
>
> (III.1.83–96)

This mixing of an older style with the playwright's own, as in
Hamlet, has the effect of making the newer style seem completely free of artifice and of dismissing the question of dramatic
adequacy.

The dramatic poetry of the mechanicals would of course remind the audience of bad verse in general—conventional details, redundancies, obvious padding, and tortured rhyme. More
particularly, it would recall the ragged couplets and wretched

quatrains that marked most plays before the regular use of blank verse. Those earlier works that have some merit, like *Damon and Pythias* or *Ralph Roister Doister,* often seem to be good in spite of the dogged poetry that muffles dramatic effectiveness and, in almost every instance, sacrifices the natural for the rhetorical. The death of Cambises is a good example:

> I feel myself a-dying now, of life bereft am I,
> And death hath caught me with his dart, for want of blood
> I spy.
> Thus gasping here on ground I lie; for nothing do I care;
> A just reward for my misdeeds my death doth plain declare.[39]

There are all sorts of difficulties here. The dying man explains that he is dying; he uses a conventional figure ("Death hath caught me with his dart") instead of stating the actual fact, that he has accidentally stabbed himself. He moralizes upon the incident and, perhaps worst of all, speaks in plodding fourteeners, straining at rhyme. The playwright thus stretches our credulity to the breaking point, and it requires only the slightest push on the parodist's part to move this kind of incident into the realm of the ridiculous once and for all:

> Now am I dead!
> Now am I fled;
> My soul is in the sky.
> Tongue, lose thy light;
> Moon, take thy flight.
> Now die, die, die, die!
> (*Midsummer Night's Dream,* V.i.306–11)

The scenes of grief and death in "Pyramus and Thisby" are, in fact, a systematic mockery of similar moments in older plays, as we can see from two that have survived, *Damon and Pythias*

39. These are Cambises' last words. The stage direction that follows them is "Here let him quake and stir." Hazlitt, *Dodsley,* p. 245.

and the anonymous *Appius and Virginia*.[40] Among the conventions for climactic scenes, apparently, was the invocation to the fates and furies. In *Damon and Pythias* we have:

> Ye Furies, all at once
> On me your torments try
>
>   . . .
>
> Gripe me, you greedy grief
> And present pangs of death,
> You sisters three, with cruel hands
> With speed come stop my breath[41]

In *Appius and Virginia* we read:

> O sisters: I search, I seek, and I crave
> No more at your hands but death for to have
>
>   . . .
>
> O gods above that rule the skies;
> Ye babes the brag in bliss:
> Ye goddesses, ye Graces, you
> What burning brunt is this?[42]

Pyramus' discovery of Thisby's mantle is plainly handled in this vein:

> Approach ye Furies fell!
> O Fates, come, come!
> Cut thread and thrum;
> Quail, crush, conclude, and quell!
>
>   (V.i.289–92)

40. *Damon and Pythias* is frequently cited as a source, but the parallels to *Appius and Virginia*, while they have not been noted, are equally impressive. Both plays clearly belong to a genre that is under attack in the *Dream*.

41. This is a song sung by Pythias, with accompaniment on the regals. Hazlitt, *Dodsley*, p. 43.

42. Ibid., pp. 144, 132.

So is Thisby's grief when her turn comes to be bereft:

> O Sisters Three!
> Come, come to me,
> With hands as pale as milk;
> Lay them in gore,
> Since you have shore
> With shears his thread of silk.
>   (V.1.343–48)

Death scenes gave, of course, an excellent opening for wild declamation. Compare Virginius, over his slain daughter, with the suicides of Pyramus and Thisby:

Vir. O cruel hands, O bloody knife, O man, what hast thou done?

Thy daughter dear and only heir her vital end hath won.

Come, fatal blade, make like dispatch: come Atropos; come, aid!

Strike home, thou careless arm, with speed: of death be not afraid.   (p. 146)

Pyr. Come, tears, confound!
>   Out, sword, and wound
> The pap of Pyramus!
>   Ay, that left pap
>   Where heart doth hop.
> Thus did I, thus, thus, thus.

.   .   .

This. Tongue, not a word!
>   Come trusty sword;
> Come blade, my breast imbrue!
>   And farewell, friends.
>   Thus Thisby ends.
> Adieu, adieu, adieu!

>   (V.1.300–05, 349–54)

We may add to this catalogue of rhetorical high points that moment when the distraught character questions the natural order and blames inanimate objects and forces for the catastrophe. Hieronimo's exclamations are typical:

> O heav'ns, why made you night to cover sin?
> By day this deed of darkness had not been.
> O earth, why didst thou not in time devour
> The vile profaner of this sacred bow'r?
>
> (Spanish Tragedy, II.5.331–34)

So too the distraught Pyramus':

> O wherefore Nature, didst thou lions frame?
> Since lion vile hath here deflow'rd my dear;
> Which is—no, no!—which was the fairest dame
> That liv'd, that lov'd, that lik'd, that look'd with cheer.
>
> (V.1.296–99)

These examples are intended not so much to identify Shakespeare's sources as to indicate the kind of conventions he was satirizing. Though he was guilty of similar posturing in *Titus Andronicus,* he had partly learned, by the time he wrote *Romeo and Juliet,* to depict a more genuine emotion in a more natural language. In later plays he goes further; Macbeth learns of his wife's death at just the moment when he might be expected to howl at the heavens, so his quiet reaction—"She should have died hereafter"—is the more effective for its breach of convention.

It is also worth remarking, as we touch upon the rhetoric of plays like *The Spanish Tragedy* and *Titus Andronicus,* that the dramatist's task of "taking the audience with him" in a rejection of older and stiffer rhetorical conventions may not have been an easy one. Shakespeare's rival theater was still presenting plays in the Senecan style if not in Cambises' vein. It was still possible in 1614, if we are to believe the prologue to *Bartholomew Fair,* to find those "who swear *Ieronimo* and *Andronicus* are the best plays yet."[43] In general, Shakespeare's purpose was better served by reference to older and less popular plays about whose ineptitude there was likely to be widespread agreement.

The parallels we can discover between the mechanicals' attempts at drama and the older plays that Shakespeare and his audiences felt they had outgrown are probably no more than glimpses of the fun that was woven into the original. We cannot recapture whatever stage business, costuming, and outright mimicry went into the performance. Nor can we do more than guess at the lost plays that may be involved. In view of the popularity of the Pyramus and Thisby legend, it seems highly probable that there had been a stage version before 1594. The only evidence of such a play, however, is a reference to a *Pyramus and Thisby* that was in the repertory of some English players who went to Germany in the train of Lord Spencer around 1603.[44] One may also wonder at Puck's curious line during the rehearsal, "A stranger Pyramus than e'er play'd here!" (III.1.90). Does "here" mean "in the woods" or does it mean, as an aside to the audience, "upon this stage"? Whether the story had been staged before or not, it was already an excellent vehicle for parody; the contemporary poetic versions, as Kenneth Muir has shown,[45] had already demonstrated that as tragedy it was dangerously inclined to the pathetic and the inadvertently comic.

The rehearsing and staging of the interlude tell much about the mechanicals' theory of the drama and even more about their practice. Again we encounter aspects of a dramaturgy familiar to Shakespeare's audience and at the same time outmoded enough to amuse them. The problems faced by Quince's com-

43. Ben Jonson, *Works,* eds. C. H. Herford and Percy Simpson (11 vols. Oxford, 1947), 6, 16.

44. Chambers, *Elizabethan Stage,* 2, 283.

45. Kenneth Muir, *Shakespeare's Sources,* 1, 31 ff.

pany and the solutions to them may be divided into three groups
—those of representation, characterization, and narration.

Behind the artisans' method of staging lies the desire to be
as realistic as possible. Thus, attempting to solve the moonlight
problem, they first resort to the almanac:

> *Quin.* Yes, it doth shine that night!
> *Bot.* Why, then you may leave a casement of the great
> chamber window, where we play, open.

> (III.1.56–59)

Quince senses that this will not do and offers a countersug-
gestion:

> Ay, or else one must come in with a bush of thorns and a
> lantern, and say he comes to disfigure, or to present, the per-
> son of Moonshine.

> (III.1.60–63)

A palpable substitute, decked out to look as much as possible
like the object in question, is the next best thing. What the
mechanicals do not realize is that such literal-mindedness actually works to destroy verisimilitude. When their device is put
to the test, the audience exposes it by quibbling in the same
literal fashion (V.1.244 ff.).

Shakespeare himself was concerned with the problem of
bringing moonlight into his play, but he solved it by relying on
poetry and trusting to the imagination of his audience. Dramatists were learning that their audiences could be counted on to
participate in the business of illusion; that they were willing,
even eager, to be deceived; and that attempts to be too realistic
were self-destructive. By showing the mechanicals erecting a
"wall" of clumsily concealed illusion, Shakespeare strengthens
the case for his own methods and his bond with the audience.

If the artisans fear that their spectators will be unable to
imagine moonlight, they also fear that, presented with a suicide

and a lion, these same spectators will be unable to react with detachment. Here they combine a touching faith in their own ability to represent reality with the assumption that their audience will be even more literal-minded than themselves. Once again they have succumbed to "realism," and in their efforts to control verisimilitude they throttle it:

> Nay, you must name his name, and half his face must be seen through the lion's neck, and he himself must speak through, saying thus, or to the same defect: "Ladies,"—or "Fair ladies."
> (III.1.35 f.)[46]

Misunderstanding of the nature of dramatic illusion can lead to more than one kind of excess. Shakespeare's fun at this point may be directed toward more than bad plays. Academic criticism had begun to invoke realism as part of a demand for the unities. Sidney professes to be very worried about verisimilitude:

> Now you shal have three Ladies walke to gather flowers, and then we must beleeve the stage to be a Garden. By and by, we heare news of shipwracke in the same place, and then wee are to blame if we accept it not for a Rock.[47]

This is the very error made by Quince and company—the assumption that drama must be taken literally or not at all. Samuel Johnson's answer to this is as firm and clearheaded as anyone could wish:

> It is false, that any representation is mistaken for reality; that any dramatic fable in its materiality was ever credible,

---

46. It has been suggested that an actual incident lies behind this, not from a play but from a royal entertainment. In 1594, a lion was removed from a triumphal procession at the Scottish court "because his presence might have brought some feare to the nearest" (New Cambridge Edition, p. 95).

47. Sir Philip Sidney, "An Apologie for Poetrie," in *Elizabethan Critical Essays,* ed. C. G. Smith (2 vols. London, 1904), *I,* 197.

or, for a single moment, was ever credited. . . . The truth is that the spectators are always in their senses and know, from the first act to the last that the stage is only a stage, and that the players are only players.[48]

While the Elizabethans were fond of anecdotes in which guilty creatures sitting at a play started up and confessed, they knew that such stories were remarkable mostly for their unlikelihood. The shared understanding of conventions and of the limitations of illusion by the dramatist and his audience made it possible for Shakespeare to poke what looks like sly fun at the unities.

The craftsmen's notion of characterization is extremely simple. Characters are types, and there are only a few. Bottom assumes that a male part is either that of a lover or a tyrant. Had he added a vice and an old man, his list would have done for most of the older dramas. But the mechanicals are striving for a kind of decorum and have no place for comic characters.

The costuming reflects their conventional approach. If Flute puts on a mask, that will suffice to make him a woman. As for Bottom, his choice is simply one of beard colors:

> I will discharge it in either your straw-color beard, your orange-tawny beard, your purple-in-grain beard, or your French-crown-colour beard, your perfit yellow.
>
> (I.2.95–98)[49]

In the interlude itself, characterization is attended to with equal sophistication. We are simply told what a particular character is like, and no discrepancy is allowed between what we are told

48. Samuel Johnson, *Samuel Johnson on Shakespeare,* ed. W. K. Wimsatt, Jr. (New York, 1960), p. 38.

49. I cannot resist quoting Johnson again: "Here Bottom discovers a true genius for the stage by his solicitude for propriety of dress, and his deliberation which beard to choose among many beards, all unnatural." Cited in Peter Alexander, *Shakespeare's Life and Art* (London, 1939), p. 108.

and what we see. In the rehearsal in the woods, Thisby characterizes Pyramus for us with a catalogue of his virtues:

> Most radiant Pyramus, most lily-white of hue,
>   Of colour like the red rose on triumphant brier,
> Most brisky juvenal, and eke most lovely Jew,
>   As true as truest horse, that yet would never tire,[50]
>   (III.1.95–98)

As a technique it is very close to the older plays. In *Appius and Virginia,* for instance, Virginius simply appears on stage at the beginning to tell us what his wife and daughter are like:

> Therefore I thank the gods above that yield to me such fate,
> To link to me so just a spouse, and eke so loving mate.
> By her I have a virgin pure, an imp of heavenly race
> Both sober, meek and modest too, and virtuous in like case.[51]

When Mater and Virginia appear, they are, true enough, a perfect wife and a virgin daughter. Their simple characterizations are set by direct statement, and nothing they say or do will alter them. They have no more psychological interest than Pyramus and Thisby and less, perhaps, than Wall and Moon and Lion.

The problems of narrative involve the mechanicals in similar difficulties. They have a story to tell, and they make what seems to be the simple task of acting it out a very complicated matter indeed. They begin with a prologue in which Quince, after

---

50. Shakespeare might almost have been parodying some of his own *Venus and Adonis:*

> "Thrice fairer than myself," she thus began,
> "The field's chief flower, sweet above compare,
> Stain to all nymphs, more lovely than a man,
> More white and red than doves or roses are."

51. Hazlitt, *Dodsley,* p. 112.

mispunctuating his apology to the audience,[52] introduces his characters and then proceeds to tell the story, giving his audience all the essential details of the plot in capsule form and with memorable rhetoric:

> Wherat, with blade, with bloody blamefull blade,
> He bravely broachd his boiling bloody breast.
>
> (V.1.145–46)

Since the plot is such a slim one, the detail of the prologue threatens to make the action superfluous. What we finally have is a play in which the main events, already anticipated, become the occasions for declamatory speeches. Rhetoric has nudged drama aside with disastrous effect. Moreover, the mechanicals are not even able to join the speeches smoothly. They think that every action must be explained, and they rely for such explanation on devices that work against dramatic effect. As the play proceeds, it is continually interrupted for this purpose:

> Then know that I one Snug the joiner am,
> A lion fell, nor else no lion's dam;
> For, if I should as lion come in strife
> Into this place, 'twere pity on my life.
>
> (V.1.226–29)

"Palpable" and "gross," Theseus' summary adjectives for the play, are accurate enough.

Thus it is that the clowns, without retracting an ounce of their clownishness, reveal a complex series of comic associations. Their taste brings to mind the worst excesses of Elizabethan verse; their notion of drama, the least successful features of a stagecraft only recently outworn; and their attempts at decorum and rhetorical glamour, the danger of preferring critical theory to practical experience and common sense. "Pyramus and

52. This device surely owes something to the mispunctuated letter in *Ralph Roister Doister*.

Thisby" calls attention to recent improvements in the dramatic
arts, an evolution experienced by audience and artist alike. The
common response of laughter at the inadequacies of the older
drama provides a dexterous means for gaining acceptance of the
new. Moreover, in the *Dream,* as in *Hamlet,* the counterpoint
between inner and outer play, old style and new style, becomes
a source of dramatic meaning. As we watch the mechanicals fail
in the art of illusion, we are temporarily diverted into accepting
the context of their failure as something more than illusion,
as real. The device leaves us with a more complex, less assured
sense of the illusion–reality relationship and leads on to one
of the major themes of the play. What we must finally say
about the sources for the mechanicals and their interlude is
that they seem to have served to strengthen and unify audience
response to the *Dream* and to open the question of the nature
and value of the art of illusion, an art for which the skills of a
carpenter, a joiner, a weaver, a tinker, and a tailor do not seem
to have sufficed.

"A Kind of History"   Christopher Sly, convinced that he is a
lord, is told that his players have arrived and are ready to play
him a comedy:

> Marry, I will; let them play it. Is not a comonty a Christmas
> gambold or a tumbling trick?
> *Lady.* No, my good lord; it is more pleasing stuff.
> *Beg.* What, household stuff?
> *Lady.* It is a kind of history.

> *(Shrew,* Ind.2.140–44)

The kind of history that was comedy had begun to flourish in
the decade preceding the composition of *A Midsummer Night's
Dream.* Thus, while Shakespeare burlesqued the tragicomedies
that had persisted from earlier times and signaled his departure
from the worst excesses of the popular stage, he had successful

models in a well-established genre upon which to draw in creating his own comedies. Two kinds of comedy had been arrived at more or less independently in the 1580s, and we may label them by their audiences as coterie comedy and popular comedy. Shakespeare was familiar with both types and, in his early comedies, appears to have been trying to unite them into a single successful prototype with the widest possible appeal.

The audience for coterie comedy was drawn from the academic world and the court. As a group, it was primed to appreciate displays of learning, literary borrowings, plots from Plautus, and, as Italian practice grew fashionable, elaborate structures of intrigue. It knew enough about literary theory to expect comedies to follow the classical and Renaissance rules. Until the time of Lyly, this kind of comedy, played in schools and universities and at the court, tended to be satirical and moralistic. Clowning and bawdiness, although they existed, had no theoretical sanction. George Whetstone, in his dedication to *Promos and Cassandra,* makes it clear that he is not interested in fun for fun's sake, but in the correction of vices. He criticizes popular comedy as "vaine, indiscreete, and out of order" and gives a summary of the elements of proper comedy:

> For, to worke a Commedie kindly, grave old men should instruct, yonge men should show the imperfections of youth, Strumpets should be lascivious, Boyes unhappy, and Clownes should speak disorderly: entermingling all these actions in such sorte as the grave matter may instruct and the pleasant delight.[53]

John Lyly developed this strain of comedy into something particularly suited to the court of Elizabeth by softening its academic qualities and playing up the court preoccupations with romantic love and classical mythology. His plays are distin-

53. Smith, *Elizabethan Critical Essays,* p. 60.

guished by short scenes in which groups of characters are introduced and then manipulated in clearly symmetrical patterns.
Starting with *Campaspe* (1584), he wrote a series of comedies
that are formal, relatively static, and full of witty, eloquent
dialogue. Characterization in his plays is never more than a
representation of abstract emotional states and moral points of
view. His Midas, for example, has three advisers: Eristus coun-
sels Midas to seek love; Martius advocates war; and Mellicrates
successfully advises the pursuit of wealth. It is very neat and
rather intellectual; the characterizations consist of little more
than reasoned speeches in defense of one or another position.
The technique is like that of the morality plays, overlaid with
Ovidian elegance. Lyly's particular strength lay in the poise and
refinement he achieved, his consistency of tone.[54]

While this was going on, the London stage continued to
present plays whose greater popularity may have derived from
their nonacademic elements—spectacular events, romantic
plots and characters, diffuse episodic structures, supernatural
happenings, and large doses of folklore. Many were adaptations
of the narrative romances, and while some could quite clearly
be called comedies, they were hardly of the type approved by the
theorists who wrote or commended the coterie comedies. They
are exactly what Whetstone was inveighing against when he
called the English playwright "out of order":

> He fyrst groundes his work on impossibilities; then in three
> howers, ronnes he throwe the worlde, marryes, gets Children,
> makes Children men, men to conquer kingdomes, murder
> Monsters, and bringeth Gods from Heaven, and fetcheth

54. Lyly was writing for boys; some of his restraint and elegance was
dictated by the special abilities and limitations of his actors. His task
was "forging a homogeneous world of dainty artifice and courtly
reticence perfectly adapted to the boys who played or the court where
they were played." G. K. Hunter, *John Lyly* (Cambridge, Mass., 1962),
p. 154.

Divels from Hel. And (that which is worst) their ground is not so unperfect as their working indiscreete: not waying, so the people laugh, though they laugh them (for their follyes) to scorne.[55]

When university men like Greene and Peele took up this kind of play, they improved its quality without really altering its structure or subject matter. Greene centered his comedies on love stories but was perfectly willing to intersperse them with clowning, magic, warfare, and intrigue. By a great stretch of the imagination, his plays may be considered "comic explorations of the nature of love,"[56] but they are so shaky in construction and so uncertain in tone that they will not stand much categorization. The phrase fits Lyly better; Greene's strength, it must be admitted, lay in his ability to maintain a continuous stream of entertainment without much regard to total harmony.

We can see the differences between coterie and popular comedy most clearly if we compare two plays that deal with similar situations. Greene's *Friar Bacon and Friar Bungay* and Lyly's first play, *Campaspe,* are founded on comparable love plots. In both plays, a ruler falls in love with a woman below his station, while she in turn falls in love with one of his subordinates. The resulting triangle forms the basic conflict of the play. The differences in execution, however, even given the contrasting settings, are enormous. In Lyly's play, the conflict gives rise to a detailed debate on the relative merits of love and honor. The tone is intellectual. In Greene's play, the same problem breeds disguises, intrigue, and suspense. The emphasis is sensational and psychological. Lyly's play has a classical setting and characters and much reference to mythology, while Greene's has an English setting and makes extensive use of folklore. The

55. Smith, p. 59.
56. R. A. Foakes, "The Comedy of Greene and Shakespeare," in *Early Shakespeare,* Stratford-upon-Avon Studies 3 (New York, 1961), p. 40.

central characters are also handled very differently. Lyly's Alexander, for all his protestations, is hardly the victim of a grand passion. He almost seems to enjoy the paradoxes into which his love leads him, and his capitulation is both graceful and magnanimous:

> *Alex.* Two loving wormes, Hephestion! I perceive Alexander cannot subdue the affections of men, though he conquer their countries. Love falls like dew aswel upon the low grasse, as upon the high Cedar. Sparkes have their heate, Antes their gall, Flyes their spleene. Well, enjoy one an other, I give her thee franckly, Apelles.[57]

Greene has little use for such euphuism in the face of a theatrical opportunity. His confrontation scene is highly melodramatic, with Prince Edward threatening the life of Lacy:

> Villain, prepare thyself; for I will bathe
> My poniard in the bosom of an earl.[58]

Only Margaret's vigorous pleading saves her lover, and Edward's final relenting is given a sort of shallow psychological validity that was not required of Alexander:

> (*aside*)   Edward, art thou that famous Prince of Wales,
> Who at Damasco beat the Saracens,
> And brought'st home triumph on thy lance's point?
> And shall thy plumes be pull'd by Venus down?
> Is't princely to dissever lovers' leagues,
> To part such friends as glory in their loves?
>   ·   ·   ·

57. *Campaspe,* in John Lyly, *Works,* ed. R. Warwick Bond (3 vols. Oxford, 1902), *4,* 357.

58. Robert Greene, "The Honourable History of Friar Bacon and Friar Bungay" in *Minor Elizabethan Drama,* ed. Ashley Thorndike (2 vols. London, 1910), 2, 191.

> Lacy, rise up. Fair Peggy, here's my hand:
> The Prince of Wales hath conquer'd all his thoughts,
> And all his loves he yields unto the earl.[59]

These events take place against very different backgrounds. Lyly fills in with the intellectual cavortings of the philosophers and their pages, not so much for a second plot as for variety and comic relief. In Greene's play, the theatrical hocus-pocus of Friar Bacon and his rival magicians and the slapstick of the servant Miles are given the status of a subplot and interwoven with the main action.

Finally, both plays offer social flattery to their respective audiences. Lyly's portrayal of Alexander suggests that power does not so much corrupt as ennoble and that rulers and aristocrats, men of worldly affairs, are really superior to philosophers. All this is prefaced and epilogued with direct appeals to the queen. Greene's play goes off in quite another direction. His Margaret, "the fair maid of Fressingfield," is morally superior to the prince who pursues her. The rustic characters in popular drama were not so much the butts of laughter as the repositories of simple country virtues. The lusty folkhero of *George A Greene* outwits a band of rebel noblemen and explains his right to strike one of them: "A poore man that is true is better than an earle, if he be false."[60] Predictably, Robin Hood appears in this play, to be bested by the heroic Pinner, reminding us that this particular strain of popular comedy has roots in the folkplays performed at fairs and on holidays at least as far back as the fifteenth century.[61]

Shakespeare's early comedies show him experimenting with

59. Ibid., p. 192.
60. Robert Greene (attr.), "A Pleasant Conceyted Comedie of George A Greene, The Pinner of Wakefield" (c. 1588), in J. Q. Adams, ed., *Chief Pre-Shakespearean Dramas* (Boston, 1924), p. 700.
61. One of the Robin Hood fragments in Adams (p. 345) can be dated before 1475.

the comic styles available through the two traditions represented by Lyly and Greene. It matters little whether he is viewed as a coterie playwright trying to reach a popular audience, like Lyly in *Mother Bombie,* or as a popular dramatist reflecting court fashions and coterie sophistication, like Peele in *The Old Wives' Tale.*[62] The point is that Shakespeare's early comedies, unlike his early history plays, seem intended, even when they fail, to capture both kinds of audience. The academic *Comedy of Errors,* modeled on Plautus and hewing to scholarly rules, is the only possible exception. It seems to belong largely to the coterie audiences, and we are not surprised by the Inns of Court performance in 1594.[63] *The Two Gentlemen of Verona,* on the other hand, is a play of divided loyalties. If, with its love versus friendship theme, it is "an elegant picture of courtly manners,"[64] it is also based on the narrative romance plot favored by popular playwrights. Its disguised heroine and its contrived and sentimental ending are reminiscent of Greene, especially of *James the Fourth.* The band of outlaws is a stock device stemming from the Robin Hood tradition. *Two Gentlemen* is undoubtedly a mixture, and a rather imperfect one.

Similar points can be made about *The Taming of the Shrew* and *Love's Labour's Lost,* although the latter is surely the most Lylyesque of Shakespeare's plays. What is more interesting in these two comedies, however, is the evidence of a developing control over audience response. Great skill and attention have been lavished on the Induction of *Shrew.* An ordinary man, persuaded that he is a lord, consents to see a play. The question

62. I know it is risky to call the author of *The Arraignment of Paris* a popular dramatist. But *David and Bethsabe* and *The Old Wives' Tale* clearly belong to the popular stage, and the latter seems to me to raise popular comedy a notch by possessing what Bradbrook calls "a greater degree of critical consciousness" (*Elizabethan Comedy,* p. 68).

63. Chambers, *Elizabethan Stage, 4,* 56.

64. Bradbrook, *Elizabethan Comedy,* p. 51.

of fashion is thus bypassed: he will see the kind of play a lord would see. What follows is an Italian-style comedy with strong folklore elements, but the audience is beyond such considerations. They have consented to watch Sly's deceivers watching Sly, who is in turn watching a comedy in which deception and "acting" proliferate rapidly. The result is a sense of simultaneous acceptance and detachment that puts aside considerations of identity in the audience; Sly, at once lord and commoner, is a good emblem for the enlarged audience that the Induction makes possible.

Despite its courtly tone, there are similar hints in *Love's Labour's Lost,* as if the playwright were uneasy about limiting himself to a particular style. There is a fuller spectrum of characters than we find in Lyly's plays and a more distinct parodistic subplot. Most significant is the fact that Shakespeare chooses to break the spell of artifice and detachment at the end, and that he is sure enough of his control to alter the course of action abruptly without damaging the consistency of the comedy.

In both of these plays, moreover, Shakespeare achieves two types of characterization that help him to synthesize his comic styles—the realist and the relevant clown. Petruchio and Biron, as unconventional men in conventional situations, offer different points of view that the audience is persuaded to share; they thus enable their respective plays to contain certain fashions without embracing them or suffering their limitations.[65] This device cuts across the normal audience divisions. Sly and Costard represent the clowns demanded in the playhouses, but they also, through their relevance to the matters at hand, meet Sidney's criticism of popular slapstick, the "extreme show of doltishness, indeed fit to lift up a loude laughter, and nothing els."[66] Doltishness was necessary to comedy; the problem was to keep it from destroying comic unity and consistency, and

65. Mercutio serves a similar purpose in *Romeo and Juliet.*
66. Smith, *Elizabethan Critical Essays,* p. 199.

Shakespeare, with these characters, was well on the way to a solution.

It was in *A Midsummer Night's Dream* that Shakespeare achieved a successful combination of elements from the two veins of popular and coterie entertainment. The remarkable variety of sources for the play can and should be viewed as evidence of a careful blending of the divergent comic styles and their conventions. That is why one-sided approaches to the play have claimed both the influence of Lyly and the influence of Greene; of court masques, entertainments, seasonal festivals, and holiday games; of the courtly audience at the marriage where it was probably first performed and the playhouse audiences that saw it later.[67] All of these claims are valid so long as they are not pushed to the exclusion of the others. The principle of amalgamation must be kept foremost.

Shakespeare's mingling is evident within groups of characters as well as among them. We may say, for instance, that the clowns belong to the tradition of popular entertainment while the Athenian lovers recall, in their relative lack of characterization and their symmetry, the *adulescens* of academic comedy and the formalized procedures of Lyly.[68] But the division, while accurate, is far from pure. The clowns' acting style and dramaturgy reflect the popular stage, but their choice of mythological subject matter reflects court fashion, and the play that they finally perform is clearly derived from the form of the antimasque.[69] The conduct of the lovers, on the other hand, does not suggest academic or Lylian practice during their night in

67. Some examples: Marco Mincoff, "Shakespeare and Lyly," *Shakespeare Survey* 14 (London, 1961), 20: "With *A Midsummer Night's Dream* comes a new advance toward Lyly, and further concessions." But see Hunter, *Lyly*, p. 330; Enid Welsford, *The Court Masque* (London, 1927); Foakes, "The Comedy of Greene and Shakespeare"; L. P. Wilkinson, *Ovid Recalled* (London, 1955), pp. 420–21.

68. George E. Duckworth, *The Nature of Roman Comedy* (Princeton, 1959), p. 242.

69. Welsford, *Court Masque*, p. 332.

the woods, where the wild activity and the continual threat of violence recall the more melodramatic strain of popular comedy.

Not all of the combinations originate with Shakespeare. Some came to him at least partially formed. Thus, while we tend to associate Theseus and Hippolyta, with their classical overtones, with the world of court comedy, they had probably already been on the stage in the *Palamon and Arcite* which the Admiral's men had performed in September of 1594.[70] The same is true of the fairies. The fashion for presenting them had sprung from the entertainments presented for Elizabeth,[71] and their first use in drama proper was probably in Lyly's *Endymion* (1588). However, Greene had already used them in *James the Fourth,* where Oberon himself brings them on to dance. Oberon also was probably familiar to the popular audiences from a dramatization of *Huon of Bordeaux.*[72]

On the whole, however, Shakespeare chooses to associate the fairies, more distinctly than the other elements in his play, with the world of court entertainment. Their entry into the play at the beginning of the second act, formal and ceremonial in its speech and movement, is extremely reminiscent of court comedy and its primary influence, the masque. The little contention between Oberon and Titania is a typical masque theme, as is its articulation, with charge and countercharge patterned as in a dance. Their language is filled with proper names that summon a remote and splendid world of mythology. Titania's long speech about the weather abounds in extravagant description; even the seasons are personified, like figures in a pageant:

> And on old Hiems' thin and icy crown
> An odorous chaplet of sweet summer buds

70. Chambers, *Elizabethan Stage, 2,* 143.

71. See John Nichols, ed., *The Progresses and Public Processions of Queen Elizabeth* (3 vols. Edinburgh and Perth, 1823), esp. *2,* 211–13; *3,* 118–19, 198 f.

72. This play was revived by Sussex' men late in 1593. See Chambers, *Elizabethan Stage, 3,* 304; *2,* 95.

> Is, as in mockery, set. The spring, the summer,
> The childing autumn, angry winter change
> Their wonted liveries.
>
> (II.1.109–13)

The same formality of staging and language is evident in the fairies' exit from the play (IV.1.69 ff.) and their reentry at the very end. Shakespeare clearly intended that his audience recognize these ritualistic elements and their origins. They serve an immediate function of separating the fairies and their world from the more mundane climate of the mortals. And, of course, they contribute to the humor by providing contrast. Bottom caught up in a masque is even funnier than Bottom among his fellow mechanicals. His scenes with Titania are enough to justify the entire fairy machinery.

Almost all of the elements of the *Dream,* as this chapter has attempted to demonstrate, can be seen as part of an attempt by the playwright to bring together divergent tendencies in the theater by working simultaneously with the preoccupations of the courtly and popular audiences. Such a synthesis had been attempted in comedy before by other playwrights and by Shakespeare himself, but *A Midsummer Night's Dream* seems to constitute a breakthrough, a completely successful wedding of elements. Material familiar and evocative enough for any audience is woven into a background that transcends, in its richness and appeal, the limitations of earlier comedies. The elements can be roughly arranged in two groups, according to their kindred associations:

Mythology	Folklore
Royal marriage	Seasonal holidays
Masques	Festival games, Pageants

Coterie theater	Popular theater
elegance and wit	clowning
metamorphosis	magic
symmetry	variety, movement
consistency	inclusiveness

Two worlds can be discerned merging easily in the *Dream*. We might call them Titania's world and Bottom's world, since she so clearly has her genealogy in the tastes and habits of the aristocratic audiences and he is so much a character who belongs to the vein of popular entertainment. Thus we can take their "marriage," temporary and delightful, as a kind of emblem for Shakespeare's achievement in this play, returning to the image with which this chapter began. It was at the magic moment when this pair met that English comedy came into its own. Here was the prancing dolt, "thrust in by the head and shoulders to play a part in majesticall matters,"[73] this time *with* decency and discretion, in the arms of the fairy queen, blessed beyond Endymion's wildest dreams. Instead of the expected incongruity there was consistency, even a sense of inevitability. We know that the achievement was very funny to everyone. We know that it helped Shakespeare reach a larger and thereafter less divided audience. We can also imagine that the audiences themselves may have had some recognition of what was being achieved in the midst of such hilarity. For some of them there must have been, along with everything else, that shock of pleasure that comes when we recognize that what is indubitably good entertainment has been subtly and successfully combined with substantial art, to the mutual enhancement of both.

73. Sidney, "An Apologie for Poetrie," p. 199.

2 ✳ The Concord of This Discord

*That the Shakespeare of the last
plays should have developed an
intense preoccupation with formal
problems, a remarkable sophistication of means, is not surprising if one
thinks of the demands on his
technical equipment during the
early years of the new century. . . .
The apparatus was fascinating in its
own right. Perhaps, if we looked
carefully for marks of this peculiar
detachment, we should find them to a
lesser degree in* As You Like It *and
in* Twelfth Night *also. . . . But
one may still think of those plays
as belonging to a time when
Shakespeare in comedy was capable
of doing extraordinary and beautiful
things* at full pressure; *the cause
of his inventions being not technical
display but the true comic theme.
And this is the sense in which one
could legitimately say that the
best of the "mature" comedies
are technically superior to all that
came later; I should myself be
prepared to maintain that*
A Midsummer Night's Dream *is
Shakespeare's best comedy.*

FRANK KERMODE

"ERRY AND TRAGICAL? TEDIOUS AND brief?" says Theseus, glancing at the mechanicals' absurd title, "That is hot ice and wondrous strange snow. / How shall we find the concord of this discord?" (V.1.58–60). It is not to be found, we soon learn, in the performance of "Pyramus and Thisby," but the concern is characteristic of Theseus, who prizes harmony in every kind of human activity. Not only does he strive to achieve it in his society; he carries it as well to his pleasures and pastimes. Melancholy is to be turned forth to funerals because it does not accord with a marriage ceremony. He has warred with Hippolyta in the past, but she is to be wed "in another key," the correct one. His hounds may be "slow in pursuit, but match'd in mouth like bells, / Each under each. A cry more tuneable / Was never holloa'd to" (IV.1.126–28). A satire is rejected because it does not "sort" with a nuptial ceremony. Finally, he is critical of the lunatic, lover, and poet because their "seething brains," while they may see more than reason sees, merely "apprehend" it, while "cool reason . . . comprehends" and thus makes reality orderly and manageable. Theseus makes a good spectator to "Pyramus and Thisby" because he "comprehends" it with sympathy and understanding, using his imagination to "amend" it.

He would not need to aid *A Midsummer Night's Dream* in the same way, for despite the enormous diversity of materials it draws upon, this comedy *finds* its concord, a unification so complete that no audience is conscious of discordant origins;

they must be ferreted out by the scholar. This chapter, then, is
for Theseus, since it attempts to show how successful the concord
of *A Midsummer Night's Dream* is and how it was achieved.
The discussion is divided between two main areas—style and
structure. It is also hoped that the examination of unity in style
and structure will tell us something of general import about
Shakespeare's dramaturgy. There are innovations in this play
that seem to be crucial to the development of his art.

STYLE

"I never heard so musical a discord"   Perhaps the first thing to
be noted about the style of *A Midsummer Night's Dream* is its
variety. If we glance through the text, our attention is caught
by the number of different verse forms and line lengths. In
addition to the prose and blank verse characteristic of any
Shakespearean drama, we find iambic pentameter couplets and
quatrains, a good deal of trochaic tetrameter, usually in couplets
but with occasional quatrains, and even some shorter lines of
two and three stresses. The mechanicals' interlude employs, however stiffly, the same rhymed measures but adds its own peculiar
stanza, an anisometric form with four dimeter and two trimeter
lines. In addition, of course, there are the songs, familiar in any
Shakespearean comedy.[1]

There are good reasons for this variation in meters and verse
forms. In the first place, it functions as a means of characterization. We associate Theseus, for example, with blank verse. It
suits his oratorical manner, and he employs it royally, measur-
ing out full verse paragraphs:

> Therefore, fair Hermia, question your desires,
> Know of your youth, examine well your blood,

---

1. There are three songs in the play (II.2.9, III.1.128, and V.1.408).
In addition, a good many passages seem to require a sort of chant, i.e.
are neither spoken naturally nor sung.

> Whether, if you yield not to your father's choice,
> You can endure the livery of a nun,
> For aye to be in shady cloister mew'd,
> To live a barren sister all your life,
> Chaunting faint hymns to the cold fruitless moon.
> Thrice blessed they that master so their blood
> To undergo such maiden pilgrimage;
> But earthlier happy is the rose distill'd
> Than that which, withering on the virgin thorn
> Grows, lives, and dies in single blessedness.
>
> (I.1.67–78)

The flexibility of blank verse as a means of characterization is demonstrated in Egeus. His use of it is very different—hurried, repetitive, the fretful exclamation of a nervous and irritable old man:

> Enough, enough, my lord! you have enough.
> I beg the law, the law, upon his head.
> They would have stol'n away; they would, Demetrius!
> Thereby to have defeated you and me—
> You of your wife and me of my consent,
> Of my consent that she should be your wife.
>
> (IV.1.157–62)

Puck, on the other hand, is "of another sort" than these mortals, so that he is often heard from in trochaic tetrameter, a measure that, by its light, skipping quality, expresses his legerity and freedom from "mortal grossness"; in several contexts it takes on a mysterious, incantatory tone:

> Now the hungry lion roars,
>   And the wolf behowls the moon;
> Whilst the heavy ploughman snores,
>   All with weary task fordone.
> Now the wasted brands do glow

> Whilst the screech owl, screeching loud,
> Puts the wretch that lies in woe
> In remembrance of a shroud.
>
> (V.1.378–85)[2]

Oberon and Titania use this measure too, but they also use fuller measures, as if to express the regality they share with Theseus and Hippolyta, of which Puck does not partake. Their blank verse and pentameter couplets match a rich, exotic diction with a lingering, almost somnolent movement:

> I know a bank where the wild thyme blows,
> Where oxlips and the nodding violets grows;
> Quite over-canopied with luscious woodbine,
> With sweet musk-roses, and with eglantine.
> There sleeps Titania sometime of the night
> Lull'd in these flowers with dances and delight.
>
> (II.1.249–54)

In addition to individual characterizations, the various meters and rhymes serve to define the groupings in *A Midsummer Night's Dream*. Thus, although the usage is by no means strict, we associate blank verse with Theseus, Hippolyta, and the courtly world at Athens; couplets with the lovers, especially as they move into the woods; lyrical measures, including song and dance, with the fairy world; and prose with the mechanicals, despite their attempts at formal verse. As various groups occupy the center of attention, we hear the particular style associated with them. One reason for this is quite practical; it enables us to follow the quickly shifting patterns of the plot, especially

2. Line 379, "beholds" in QqFf, was amended by Warburton to "behowls," and subsequent editors have accepted the reading. Since there are several other sounds evoked in the passage, however, it might be held that "behowls" is overdoing it and that the silent picture of the wolf is at least as effective.

during the night of errors in the woods. We are acclimated to each turn of events by a stylistic change.

The stylistic shifts serve to point up important themes as well. As they take us from one group of characters to the next, one setting to the next, they begin to make us aware of the play's strong contrasts—day and night, mortal and fairy, city and woods. These lead us in turn to more abstract sets of opposites like illusion and reality or, as in the mechanicals' rehearsal described above, the natural qualities of the craftsmen and the artificial qualities of their interlude—art versus nature.

The transitions, with their accompanying interplay of contrasts, can be extremely subtle. In the first scene, for example, Hermia and Lysander, left alone by the others, continue to use the blank verse that began the play. They are permitted a brief and charming conversation about the vicissitudes true lovers must endure. The scene ends, however, with the arrival of Helena and some necessary, but rather artificial, plot business: Helena's irrational decision to inform Demetrius of their flight. This is far better rendered in the more formal couplets that are used throughout to accompany the patterned and mechanical behavior of the four lovers.[3] Already then, before Helena's arrival, the conversation has begun to take on more formal qualities (I.1.135–40). Just before Helena's entrance, Hermia begins to speak in couplets, so that her arrival and the couplet scene that follows are prepared for gradually and effectively.

Conversely, when the playwright wants strong contrast, he uses it. The first of the mechanicals' scenes is sandwiched between the one just discussed and our introduction to the fairies, so that we move rather abruptly from Helena's decorous cou-

---

3. In general, the lovers resort more and more to couplets as they get further into the "woods" of confusion. At the climax of their troubles, however, genuine emotion breaks out, especially between the women (who have not had the love-juice), and they go back to blank verse for a time (III.2.195 f.).

plets to Bottom's exuberant and error-ridden prose, and, at the end of the scene, from Bottom's expectation of rehearsing "obscenely and courageously" to the lyric that opens the second act, the "amphimacers" whose delicacy Coleridge so greatly admired.[4] That lyric, on the other hand, shifts smoothly into the couplet dialogue of the fairy and Puck, moving to pentameter by way of some tetrameter couplets that, in turn, alter from trochaic to iambic. All of this then merges gracefully into the blank verse passages between Oberon and Titania. And so the play goes.

The variety of styles in this play and the frequently alternating use of them, despite their success and the careful control that has obviously been exercised over them, have frequently called forth strictures from commentators and have even been used to cast doubt on the play's authenticity. Discussions of the lovers, for instance, almost always produce comments to the effect that they are poorly characterized, difficult to tell apart, puppets who speak in couplets that are artificial to the point of absurdity.[5] This, it is often remarked, is evidence of Shakespeare's dramatic immaturity; later on, he will learn to provide fuller characterizations and less stilted dialogue.

Such criticism does not do justice to the integrity and unity of *A Midsummer Night's Dream,* nor does it accord with the dramatist's skill as exhibited elsewhere in the play. The four lovers, after all, *are* puppets while they are in the woods, the helpless victims of supernatural enchantments. Their state is pointed up and made amusing by the artificiality of their move-

---

4. Criticizing Theobald's reading ("through" in Q2Ff rather than "thorough" in Q1), Coleridge remarked: "The eight amphimacers have so delightful an effect on the ear! and then the sweet transition to the trochaic" (Samuel Taylor Coleridge, *Coleridge's Shakespearean Criticism,* ed. T. M. Raysor [2 vols. London, 1930], *1,* 100–01).

5. "It is a commonplace that the lovers of MND are but faintly sketched and barely differentiated" (Arden Edition, p. 23).

ments and their speech. Were they more fully characterized we
would develop an interest in and sympathy for them which the
pace of the play does not allow, and the detachment that we
need to laugh at their misfortunes would be threatened. Here,
for example, is Hermia at a moment very close to despair:

> Never so weary, never so in woe;
>> Bedabbled with the dew, and torn with briers;
> I can no further crawl, no further go;
>> My legs can keep no pace with my desires.
> Here will I rest me till the break of day.
> Heavens shield Lysander, if they mean a fray!
>
>   (III.2.442–47)

Having said this, she immediately goes to sleep among the
other three lovers. Our attention rests not on her despair but
on the completion of a formal movement directed by Robin
Goodfellow and the comic discrepancy between what Hermia
thinks is going on and what we know to be the truth. "Briers"
and "desires" both have serious potential, but paired in a rhyme
they maintain the formal and comic tone. The playwright is
clearly in control of our response. To demand that the lovers
speak and act more naturally is to demand a different plot and
a different play.

Artificiality is the means of achieving aesthetic distance
throughout *A Midsummer Night's Dream,* and Shakespeare
proves himself perfectly capable, when he wishes, of closing
the gaps he has deliberately opened up by the use of formal
styles and patterns of incident. The first scene, cited above, is a
good example of this careful control of style for dramatic effect.
Helena, upon her entrance, speaks of her wish to imitate Hermia
in order to regain Demetrius' favor:

> Sickness is catching. O, were favour so,
> Yours would I catch, fair Hermia, ere I go!

My ear should catch your voice, my eye your eye,
My tongue should catch your tongue's sweet melody.
                                        (I.1.186–89)

The irony here is that just before Helena's entrance Hermia,
who had been speaking blank verse, falls into couplets with the
swearing of her love-oath. It is into *this* world that Helena
comes to be held prisoner. The two women's "tongues" are not
so different as they think; both are caught up in the artificial
crisis of love that is not to be resolved until the sun rises on
Theseus' wedding day. Until then, all four lovers are condemned
to a less natural and less eloquent language, one that mirrors the
absurdity of their dilemma and the relative lack of personality
forced on them by "love-in-idleness." In its easily dismissable
formality, the style also prophesies the happy conclusion of
their desires.

The play's variations of style have also been cited to make a
case for its extensive revision. John Dover Wilson and Sir
Arthur Quiller-Couch, in their Cambridge edition of the play,
demonstrate convincingly that mislineations in the blank verse
of the Quarto (at V.1.1–84) indicate that it was set from a manuscript in which textual additions were written in the margin
in a fashion that made their lineation unclear. Wilson goes on
to maintain that the difference in quality between the old lines
and the additions is great enough to suggest that the former
were "early Shakespearian verse" and the latter "mature Shakespearian verse."[6] This does not, as Chambers points out, necessarily follow:

In 5.1.1–84 correctly lined passages alternate with others
which are mislined, and I agree with Wilson that the latter
probably represent additional matter written without lineation in the margin of the manuscript. They are a little more

6. New Cambridge Edition, pp. 80–86, 141–42.

freely written than the original lines which they supplement. This hardly excludes the possibility that they were afterthoughts at the time of original composition.[7]

Wilson is not interested in the possibility that the playwright might have sketched out the scene and then gone back at leisure to fill it in, or even in the supposition that the added lines were only a year or two away from the original. To him the difference in their quality is too great. He particularly objects to Theseus' final couplet, "Or in the night, imagining some fear, / How easy is a bush suppos'd a bear!" (V.1.21–22), approvingly quoting R. G. White, who had thought the lines an interpolation:

> Would Shakespeare, after thus reaching the climax of his thought, fall a-twaddling about bushes and bears? Note too the loss of dignity in the rhythm. I cannot even bring myself to doubt that these lines are interpolated.[8]

The first point to be made about this comment is that White has ignored the dramatic context. It is not Shakespeare's thought we are speaking of, but Theseus'; if anyone is twaddling or losing dignity it is not the author, but his character. But *is* anyone twaddling? What Theseus says is germane to the rest of his speech and to the rest of the play, as well as to his characterization.[9] The loss of dignity of which White speaks is probably the shift from blank verse to couplet. Such a shift is, as we have seen, very characteristic of the play. All but one of Theseus' longer speeches in the fourth and fifth acts end with couplets. Do Wilson and White wish to remove these too? Should all the couplets in the play be doubted on the grounds that they lack dignity?

7. Chambers, *William Shakespeare, 1,* 360.
8. New Cambridge Edition, pp. 141–42.
9. G. Wilson Knight, *The Shakespearean Tempest* (London, 1932), pp. 151–53, shows that the words "bush" and "bear" are integral to the imagery of the play.

Some critics of the play go almost that far. Wilson's doubts are pushed further by Walter de la Mare in an essay that suggests that most of the scenes between the lovers were by a hand other than Shakespeare's. All of the speeches that he cites as unworthy of Shakespeare are in couplets. He calls them "shallow, stumbling, bald, and vacant"; compared to Titania's speeches, which are "poetry in essence," these are merely poetical "in tincture."[10] It is surely more profitable to compare different speeches by the same character or even within the same character-group, since we do not expect all the characters in the play to sound alike or to speak "poetry in essence." De la Mare does compare two speeches by Egeus, calling one genuine and the other spurious, but not, I think, convincingly. He then poses two interesting rhetorical questions:

> Can we recall any other play written at one time and by one author that reveals discords in style and inequalities of mere intelligence so extreme? Did ever a fine poet indeed—let alone that pre-eminent prince of poets, Shakespeare—when once his imagination and his gift of expression had come of age, thus indulge, now in excellent, and now in dull and characterless verse?[11]

To dispose of the last question first, the answer is certainly yes, most poets, even great poets, are very uneven all of their lives. Wordsworth might be cited or Tennyson or, for that matter, de la Mare himself. Further, the question, like White's strictures, ignores the conditions of drama. If Shakespeare had been responsible merely for writing good poetry, *A Midsummer Night's Dream* would have been different. In answer to the first question, I would cite the plays written around the time of *A Midsummer Night's Dream—Romeo and Juliet* and *Rich-*

10. Walter de la Mare, *Pleasures and Speculations* (London, 1940), p. 294.
11. Ibid., p. 295.

ard II. Both have the same features that de la Mare considers discords in style and inequalities of intelligence, that is, in both plays, Shakespeare uses formal and somewhat conventional verse patterns to achieve certain dramatic effects. Does not *The Tempest,* for that matter, have its artificial moments and its "unpoetical" language?

Wilson supports de la Mare's dismemberment of the play in a 1948 essay, reprinted in his recent *Shakespeare's Happy Comedies,*[12] so we may assume that the theory is still current. Both critics, it seems to me, approach the play with a romantic attitude: because of its beautiful poetry, they wish it to be *all* poetry—perhaps in the manner of Herrick's fairy poems—to purge it, as Titania would Bottom, of "mortal grossness." But the language to which they object has a dramatic validity. The couplets de la Mare quotes are genuinely funny in performance, and this is partly because of their mechanical tone; they emphasize the unnatural behavior of people who think they are acting naturally. De la Mare sees them as without humor and finds that they lack the verbal music he associates with Shakespeare. There have always been those who seem to wish that Shakespeare had abandoned drama and concentrated on writing pure poetry (despite the evidence of his poems), and there has always been a tendency, because of its array of styles, to extract from and disjoint *A Midsummer Night's Dream.*[13]

It was suggested at the outset that we might find in this study of the style and structure of the play important innovations tak-

12. Wilson relegates *Midsummer Night's Dream* to the back of this book, treating it only in terms of its "problems"—dating, sources, revision.

13. Seventeenth- and eighteenth-century performances almost always used only one section of the play. Oddly enough, Robertson, the archdisintegrationist, thought *Dream* the only play in the canon completely by Shakespeare. He also thought it "juvenile, fantastic, unvital, turning on fairy tricks and cross-purposes" (J. M. Robertson, *Montaigne and Shakespeare* [London, 1909], p. 237).

ing their place in the practice of Shakespeare's art. What are we
to say of the device of stylistic variety? It is certainly true that
the plays of the same period as the *Dream*—*Romeo and Juliet,
Love's Labour's Lost,* the two *Richards*—show an extensive and
developing use of different verse styles employed for dramatic
meaning and effect. Did Shakespeare later abandon the device
because he found better ways of achieving the same effects? I
think not, although his use of stylistic diversity certainly became more subtle. If we think of the way in which varied styles
are juxtaposed to achieve the playwright's ends in *Henry IV* and
Hamlet, we will have a sense both of his continuity of technique and the modifications it underwent. To consider couplets
and other kinds of verbal formality only as signs of immaturity
in the playwright would be to miss this aspect of his development and blind ourselves to his purpose in using them.

"How comes this gentle concord in the world?"   If Shakespeare
created a multitude of styles for purposes of characterization and
contrast in *A Midsummer Night's Dream,* he also took pains to
combine them in a way that reconciles them. His problem with
such an omnium-gatherum of materials and characters, after all,
was not the achievement of diversity; it was the need for con-
solidation, for the attainment of an organic unity "more tune-
able than lark to shepherd's ear." For such a task the dramatist
called on every stylistic and structural device he could muster.

We may begin with the iterative imagery to which a suc-
cession of critics have called attention in the past thirty years—
the strong sense of night and darkness that the play engenders;
the recurrent attention to stars, moon, moonlight, and water;
and the accompanying imagery of dissension and nightmare,
beasts and birds, and jewels and music.[14] Such intricate play of

14. F. C. Kolbe, *Shakespeare's Way* (London, 1930); G. Wilson
Knight, *The Shakespearean Tempest;* C. F. Spurgeon, *Shakespeare's
Imagery and What It Tells Us* (London, 1936); Wolfgang Clemen,
Shakespeare's Bilder (Bonn, 1936); Mark Van Doren, *Shakespeare*
(New York, 1939).

imagery is, of course, everywhere characteristic of Shakespeare, but the *Dream* may be counted among the first plays, along with *Richard II* and *Romeo and Juliet,* to use it consistently and with full success. The image patterns in *Love's Labour's Lost,* as Miss Spurgeon points out, appear to be applied to the play as decoration.[15] This is not the case with *A Midsummer Night's Dream.* Its moon is of the very essence and texture of the play; we could no more root it out of the play's language than we could chop down the woods. It grows naturally out of the subject matter of love, lunacy, and midsummer night and becomes the essential setting of the play and the source by which we are made aware of such themes as illusion, disorder, and imagination. As such, it remains a perfect example of Shakespeare's most effective use of the iterative image.

Other unifying features of *A Midsummer Night's Dream* have not received the kind of critical attention lavished on its imagery. To one of these I would give the label "picturization." Again and again, we are given not merely the glimpse afforded by an image, but a fully drawn picture. Often, these are sketches of human activity. Thus, before the play has gone very far, Egeus has given us a picture of Lysander courting; Theseus has sketched for Hermia the life of a nun; Bottom has demonstrated, since he is not capable of describing, the way a tyrant rants; Puck has shown us a gossip drinking from a bowl and an aunt falling from her stool; and Titania has pictured Oberon, disguised as Corin, piping to "amorous Phillida." These pictorial effects slow down the action; but in their evocation of

15. Spurgeon, *Imagery,* pp. 271–73. Miss Spurgeon makes an odd remark at this point: "Only in three of the comedies do we find slight traces of the running symbolical imagery, used as in the tragedies, to illustrate or underline a leading 'motive' in the action or plot of the play, and these three are *Love's Labour's Lost, Much Ado,* and *All's Well"* (p. 271). Either her discussion of the moon imagery in the *Dream* has slipped her mind, or she fails to see its connection with the themes of love, imagination, madness, illusion, fertility, and metamorphosis, all of them leading "motives" in the action of the play. The remark is unjust to other comedies as well.

the imagination, their illustrations of its follies, triumphs, and possibilities, they realize the play's basic theme in a new and significant dimension.

The most effective and memorable pictures in the play are not the glimpses of single figures and activities described above. They are the larger representations, full landscapes with a remarkable sense of spaciousness and distance. These we might call "panoramas." While we catch initial hints of them in Theseus' picture of his wedding with all of Athens reveling and in the poignant conversation between Hermia and Lysander that follows, they do not really begin to dominate the play until the entrance of the fairies in the second act. Then, they appear in profusion. Titania's fairy starts things with an extensive answer to Puck's "Whither wander you?" He counters by summoning up all the places where Oberon and Titania have quarreled over the changeling boy. Titania and Oberon take it up, she with a reference to "the farthest steep of India," he with a glimpse of her leading Theseus "through the glimmering night / From Perigouna, whom he ravished." The queen then begins her long and Bruegelesque[16] summary of the trouble they have caused in the natural world:

> These are the forgeries of jealousy:
> And never, since the middle summer's spring,

16. Landscape painting was hardly flourishing in England at the time the play was written. It is interesting, however, to compare the styles of the Flemish landscapists of the period, which contain similarities to the verbal panorama of the *Dream*. See, for instance, Bruegel, "Landscape with the parable of the Sower" (1556), Philadelphia Museum of Art, ill. in F. Grossman, *Bruegel* (2 vols. London, 1955), *1*, pl. 5; Lucas van Valkenborch, "Spring" (also called "Picnic with Elegant Company") (1587), Vienna Kunsthistorisches Museum, ill. in *Katalog der Gemäldegalerie*, Pt. II, no. 384 (1958), pl. 46; Abraham Govaerts, "A Forest Scene" ("Oakwood with Gypsies") (1612), The Hague, ill. in R. H. Wilenski, *Flemish Painters* (2 vols. London, 1960), *2*, pl. 478; also see pl. 464–67, 473, 476–77, and 479.

Met we on hill, in dale, forest, or mead,
By paved fountain or by rushy brook,
Or in the beached margent of the sea,
To dance our ringlets to the whistling wind,
But with thy brawls thou hast disturb'd our sport.
Therefore the winds, piping to us in vain,
As in revenge, have suck'd up from the sea
Contagious fogs; which falling in the land
Hath every pelting river made so proud
That they have overborne their continents.
The ox hath therefore stretch'd his yoke in vain,
The ploughman lost his sweat, and the green corn
Hath rotted ere his youth attain'd a beard;
The fold stands empty in the drowned field,
And crows are fatted with the murrion flock;
The nine men's morris is fill'd up with mud;
And the quaint mazes in the wanton green
For lack of tread are undistinguishable.

(II.1.81–100)

She goes on to include the different seasons and describe their confusion. Above it all, of course, "the moon, the governess of floods, / Pale in her anger, washes all the air." Then, as if she had not been exhaustive enough in her cross section of geography, weather, and natural life, Titania presents in her next speech a seascape, with herself and her "votaress" in the foreground and the "embarked traders on the flood" in the distance.

Oberon is not to be outdone at this activity. After his wife has presented her sweeping panoramas for us and left the stage, he has his turn; he even gives us a vantage point for the next great view:

My gentle Puck, come hither. Thou rememb'rest
Since once I sat upon a promontory
And heard a mermaid, on a dolphin's back,

> Uttering such dulcet and harmonious breath
> That the rude sea grew civil at her song,
> And certain stars shot madly from their spheres
> To hear the sea-maid's music.
>
> (II.1.148–54)

"I remember," answers Puck, and we pause to regain control of our dizzying imaginations. But Oberon will not let us rest. He moves on to a vision of even greater proportions:

> That very time I saw (but thou couldst not)
> Flying between the cold moon and the earth,
> Cupid, all arm'd. A certain aim he took
> At a fair Vestal, throned by the West,
> And loos'd his love-shaft smartly from his bow,
> As it should pierce a hundred thousand hearts.
> But I might see young Cupid's fiery shaft
> Quench'd in the chaste beams of the wat'ry moon,
> And the imperial vot'ress passed on,
> In maiden meditation, fancy free.
> Yet mark'd I where the bolt of Cupid fell.
> It fell upon a little Western flower;
> Before, milk-white, now purple with love's wound,
> And maidens call it, love-in-idleness.
>
> (II.1.155–68)

We come finally to rest on something small and familiar, the pansy.

Throughout the night in the woods that follows, confined and hectic as it may be, we get echoes and glimpses of these magnificent views and distances. Oberon's description of the bank where Titania sleeps among the flowers is a smaller panorama, but it has its own sweep and detail. Hermia, as if responding to the fairies' talk of girdling the earth (II.1.175) and compassing the globe (IV.1.100), imagines the moon creeping through a hole bored in the earth and emerging on the other side to shine on the Antipodes (III.2.52–55). Puck, searching for distance in his description of the fleeing mechanicals, widens the prospect:

> As wild geese that the creeping fowler eye,
> Or russet-pated choughs, many in sort,
> Rising and cawing at the gun's report,
> Sever themselves and madly sweep the sky;
> So at his sight away his fellows fly.
>
> (III.2.20–24)

Even Demetrius, in a flight of passion, can transport us to the mountains of Asia and "That pure congealed white, high Taurus snow, / Fann'd with the eastern wind" (III.2.141–42).

As daylight returns to the play, the panoramas regain full splendor. First there is Puck's warning of the approaching dawn, with its clouds, shining sky, churchyards, crossways, and floods; then Oberon's answer, a brilliant depiction of sunrise over the sea. Theseus' speech, as he enters the play with full daylight, is in the same vein. He is on his way to arrange a panorama of sight and sound:

> And since we have the vaward of the day,
> My love shall hear the music of my hounds.
> Uncouple in the western valley; let them go.
> Dispatch, I say, and find the forester.
> We will, fair Queen, up to the mountain's top
> And mark the musical confusion
> Of hounds and echo in conjunction.
>
> (IV.1.108–14)

Hippolyta responds with a spacious description of a similar event when Hercules and Cadmus "bay'd the bear" in "a wood of Crete," and "the groves, / The skies, the fountains, every re-

gion near / Seem'd all one mutual cry." We are certainly prepared by all these vistas for Demetrius' wondering comment
on the night in the woods:

> These things seem small and undistinguishable,
> Like far-off mountains turned into clouds.
>
> (IV.1.190–91)

The last full panorama in the play comes at Puck's entrance in
the fifth act, a night scene with lion, wolf, snoring ploughman,
screech-owl, insomniac, gaping graves, and spirits gliding on
the churchway paths, the whole coming to rest at the place of
performance, "this hallowed house" (V.1.378–95).

The function of these panoramas is not difficult to discern.
They provide, as suggested above, a contrast to the confinement
of the woods, escorting us in and drawing us out again. They
create perspective and distance, both in the geographic and
aesthetic senses of those words. Through them, we are made
aware of both man's pettiness and his grandeur, simultaneous
extremes that are also expressed through the fairies. Only such
comprehensive vantage points could give us this sense of survey-
ing all of nature in order to discover man's unique position in it.

In their richness and variety, the panoramas become a kind of
metaphor for the play: *A Midsummer Night's Dream* is itself
a panorama of smaller scenes and characters, a great landscape
with cities, woods, fields, mountains, valleys, rivers, ocean, and
a host of figures representative of society and the supernatural.
Theseus' "The best in this kind are but shadows" and Puck's "No
more yielding but a dream" take on a perspective of their own
when we can link them to Demetrius' "These things seem small
and undistinguishable, / Like far-off mountains turned into
clouds." Even our initial sense of wonder at these flights of
description has its function. C. L. Barber touches on this when,
defending the "autonomous bravura passages" in the play, he
remarks that they are "calculated to make the audience respond

with wonder to the effortless reach of imagination which brings the stars madly shooting from their spheres."[17] Like the patterns of imagery, the panoramas contribute significantly to the play's atmosphere of magic, spaciousness, and limitless possibility, all attributes of the power of imagination which it both derives from and celebrates.

Another unifying characteristic of the style of *A Midsummer Night's Dream* is its profusion. Elizabeth Sewell, analyzing the play as "natural history," writes:

> Anyone who is interested may try an experiment with this play: Begin at the beginning and note down references to natural phenomena as they occur. The experimenter will almost certainly be exhausted before getting halfway through. The profusion is astonishing.[18]

This profusion is achieved by the simplest and most direct stylistic means available—listing. Again and again, the characters in the play refuse to content themselves with mentioning one or two events, objects, or contingencies; they break into a list, as if to exahust every possibility. Egeus is not content to say that Lysander has exchanged love tokens with Hermia; he must name them all:

> bracelets of thy hair, rings, gauds, conceits,
> Knacks, trifles, nosegays, sweetmeats . . .
>
> (I.1.33–34)

This is not merely the garrulity of an old man. Every character in the play has the same habit. Lysander and Hermia list all the obstacles to love—blood, years, friends, war, death, and sick-

17. Barber, *Shakespeare's Festive Comedy*, p. 148.
18. Elizabeth Sewell, *The Orphic Voice: Poetry and Natural History* (New Haven, 1960), p. 121.

ness (I.1.135–42); Puck and the fairy, when they meet, list the places they haunt and then go on to Goodfellow's activities:

> Are you not he
> That frights the maidens of the villagery;
> Skim milk, and sometimes labour in the quern,
> And bootless make the breathless housewife churn;
> And sometime make the drink to bear no barm;
> Mislead night-wanderers, laughing at their harm?
> Those that Hobgoblin call you, and sweet Puck,
> You do their work, and they shall have good luck.
> Are you not he?
>
> (II.1.34–42)

The answer to this, of course, is not simply yes, but another list to match it. Titania, as we have seen, lists geographical features, meteorological phenomena, and the seasons. Before she goes to sleep, her fairies sing a song naming all the creatures who are not to disturb her. Oberon, on the other hand, is interested in the beasts who *might* disturb her and with whom she thus might fall in love. He lists them—lion, bear, wolf, bull, meddling monkey, busy ape—when he first hatches his plot (II.1.180) and again—ounce, cat, bear, pard, boar with bristled hair—as he squeezes the juice on her eyelids (II.2.30). He also enumerates the flowers among which she sleeps (II.1.249 f.). Theseus lists the activities of the imagination (V.1.9 f.) and reads a list of proffered entertainments. Even Bottom is a tabulator. He urges Quince to list the actors and the parts (I.2.2 f.); he enumerates the beards he might wear (I.2.95 f.); and his charming third-act song is a kind of roll call of birds:

> The woosel cock so black of hue,
>   With orange-tawny bill,
> The throstle with his note so true,
>   The wren with little quill—

The finch, the sparrow, and the lark,
    The plain-song cuckoo gray,
Whose note full many a man doth mark,
    And dares not answer nay.
                        (III.1.128–36)

Perhaps it is easier for Titania to fall in love with Bottom while
he is listing these creatures, for she and the other fairies, including Puck, are the best cataloguers in the play. It was with
Titania's speech in III.1.167 ("Be kind and courteous to this
gentleman") that Miss Sewell gave up counting the references to
natural phenomena because, as she says, "in six or seven lines the
listmaker suddenly and finally disappears from sight under
showers of apricocks and figs and dewberries, not to mention
honey and butterflies and bees and glow-worms."[19]

What is the meaning of all these tallies and inventories? Part
of it can be attributed to the Elizabethan love of rhetorical am-
plitude, the habit of piling up examples and surrounding an
idea with an array of illustration. Lyly did it with elegance;
Nashe, with pungency. But the abundance achieved by listing
is especially striking in *A Midsummer Night's Dream,* and it
contributes to the play some of its most memorable moments.
We can see that, like the panoramas, the lists work constantly
to widen possibility, to suggest further objects, creatures, places,
and events. Moreover, like the reiterated images they serve to
create a fully realized world. The moon imagery brings the
moonlight, but the lists of beasts, birds, flowers, and features of
the landscape create a strong sense of encountering nature in
all its prolix immediacy. Here is the imagination again, attempting to comprehend everything available to it, pouring forth a
cornucopia of sensuous experience that threatens either to
drown us in its profusion or widen our horizons. Here variety
and unity are simultaneously expressed.

19. Sewell, *The Orphic Voice,* p. 121.

Listing, then, is one way of bringing an audience seated in a theater into contact with nature, stimulating and awakening the sensuous memory. Shakespeare was to use the device again, most notably in *Lear,* a play profoundly concerned with nature. Poor Tom's diet, with its wealth of uncomfortably explicit details, will serve to illustrate the listing in that play:

> Poor Tom, that eats the swimming frog, the toad, the tadpole, the wall-newt and the water; that in the fury of his heart, when the foul fiend rages, eats cow dung for sallets, swallows the old rat and the ditch-dog, drinks the green mantle of the standing pool; who is whipp'd from tithing to tithing, and stock-punish'd and imprison'd; who hath had three suits to his back, six shirts to his body.
>
> (III.4.134 f.)

Often in *Lear,* as in the *Dream,* listing is a response, an opportunity seized by one character to elaborate on what has been said by another. When Lear imagines that dogs are barking at him, Edgar responds with a beggar's charm against dogs:

> Mastiff, greyhound, mongrel grim,
> Hound or spaniel, brach or lym,
> Bobtail tyke or trundle-tail—
> Tom will make them weep and wail.
> (III.6.71–74)

The charm suggests an association of listing and magic, a relationship which will be more obvious if we recall the recitations and incantations associated with the performance of magic and the important roles played by naming and listing in primitive religions. Shakespeare's other magic plays, *Macbeth, The Winter's Tale,* and *The Tempest,* are notable for their lists too; in *The Tempest* they have the same incantatory quality (e.g. the famous speech in V.1.33 f. which begins "Ye elves of hills, brooks, standing lakes and groves") that we find in the *Dream* at those moments when the fairies are performing magic and ritual blessing. The magician, when he names and lists, is "summoning." The dramatist's activity is kindred; he too is summoning nature to his stage in all of its profusion, power, and mystery.

Though the discussion thus far has concentrated on the play's richness, justice would not be done if we did not note in it, in conclusion, an opposite impulse toward directness and simplicity. Here, for contrast, is a specimen of listing from *Love's Labour's Lost:*

> O, never will I trust to speeches penn'd,
>   Nor to the motion of a schoolboy's tongue,
> Nor never come in vizard to my friend,
>   Nor woo in rhyme, like a blind harper's song!
> Taffeta phrases, silken terms precise,
>   Three-pil'd hyperboles, spruce affectation,
> Figures pedantical—these summer flies
>   Have blown me full of maggot ostentation.
>   (V.2.402–09)

There is no language of this kind in *A Midsummer Night's Dream,* not even from the lovers. "Maggot ostentation," even as evidence of folly, has been abandoned. The lists are simple and concrete; the imagery rises naturally from the action; the panoramas are composed of sharp and realistic details. Bottom can converse with the fairies successfully because both speak in particulars and with vocabularies that meet; he is not, like Costard, the bewildered spectator of a fireworks display of witty language. B. Ifor Evans, who admires the simple and direct language of the *Dream,* speaks of it as "one of the most original and balanced plays in all Shakespeare's work."[20] The originality lies partly in the remarkable range of style and the balance in

20. B. Ifor Evans, *The Language of Shakespeare's Plays* (Bloomington, Ind., 1952), pp. 49–50.

the integration of style with total dramatic effect. In this play, Shakespeare's style seems to be capable of almost any feat, from the most formal to the most relaxed effects, from the artificial to the natural, the direct to the elaborate, the lyrical to the mundane. What is more important, however, is that we are hardly conscious of it as style or inclined to distinguish it from other aspects of dramatic excellence. All the stylistic effects are harmonized; they form a concord, and that concord joins the larger whole that is the play.

STRUCTURE

"The iron tongue of midnight hath told twelve"   The structure of *A Midsummer Night's Dream* involves, among other things, its time scheme, long considered a problem. The difficulties are well known; temporal references in the play are, like the references to the moon, inconsistent. Theseus and Hippolyta, at the beginning of the play, expect to wait four days until their marriage ceremony; count as they will, however, commentators are able to account for only three. There are various ways in which this discrepancy may be explained. It can be argued that Theseus and Hippolyta succumb to their impatience and move things up one day, or that everyone is anxious to seal the bonds between the quartet of lovers while they are harmoniously arranged. It is also quite possible that the occasion of the original performance was, in fact, four days before the wedding of the couple honored by the play and that Shakespeare never bothered to readjust this actual reference to the details of the plot. The discrepancies in the time scheme have also been used to support theories of revision. But the most sensible reaction is that of Kittredge:

> The time scheme of the drama has worried the critics a good deal and has helped them in spinning tenuous theories of revision. We need only observe that the four days and four

nights contemplated by Hippolyta in I, i, 7–11, are not fully spanned. . . . No audience would note the discrepancy, for the night in the enchanted forest is long enough to bewilder the imagination.[21]

Hippolyta supports this when she says:

> Four days will quickly steep themselves in night;
> Four nights will quickly dream away the time.
>
> (I.1.7–8)

The time in this play is indeed "dreamed away," so that undue concern about its exact chronology is a little like the mechanicals' anxious consultation of the almanac.

The temporal patterning of the play is more profitably examined in terms of its effect on the audience. What they witness is a movement from daytime in the city to nighttime in the woods, which then swings back to day again. All of this is controlled by the dramatist in a way that leaves no confusion about the time of day or night at any given moment in the play.[22] We are carefully prepared for the nocturnal scenes first by the planning of the lovers, then by the rehearsal arrangements of the clowns. In the first night-scene at the opening of the second act, we are brought gradually to an awareness of night which is very like the gathering of dusk on a summer evening. There are oblique references in the opening lines to the moon, night, and starlight; these are balanced by visual images that do not suggest darkness. Puck next describes himself as a "wanderer of the night" and sketches two indoor nocturnal scenes. With Oberon's entrance and opening line—"Ill met by moonlight, proud Titania"—we have come to full night, but it is and will

---

21. Kittredge Edition, p. ix.

22. Cf. the discussion of scene-setting techniques in this play in Arthur Colby Sprague, *Shakespeare and His Audience: A Study in the Technique of Exposition* (Cambridge, Mass., 1935), pp. 56 f.

remain, for the most part, the peculiarly "glimmering" night which Oberon mentions a few lines later.

Similarly, we begin to anticipate the arrival of daylight long before it comes. "Cock crow" has been mentioned before the end of the second act. The end of the third act brings Puck's "this must be done with haste" speech and Oberon's reply, which fully prepares us for dawn. We have one more scene, however, before daybreak, that between Bottom and Titania. Then, with all the necessary magic performed, the fairies "hear the morning lark" and leave the stage; a horn blows, and Theseus and Hippolyta enter, bringing with them full daylight. This day-night-day pattern is all the audience knows and all it needs to know.

Almost all, one should say, for the play takes one more turn back to darkness again, and the pattern becomes day-night-day-night. We are vaguely aware of this throughout the fifth act because Theseus has mentioned the need to while away the space between "after-supper and bedtime," a matter of some three hours. The "tedious brief" scene of Pyramus and Thisby, as if to make its oxymoron come true, takes up this time, for as it ends Theseus announces that it is past midnight. This is an excellent example of Shakespeare's illusory use of time for dramatic effect. It may not be credible to the scrupulous commentator that "Pyramus and Thisby" could occupy three hours, but it is perfectly credible to the audience, even though Theseus' announcement comes as something of a jolt. The jolt has a dramatic function, for the audience has nearly forgotton the fairies and their world. The lovers may think that they are out of the woods and free for good of their midsummer madness, but the audience is to be reminded that error, illusion, and mystery still exist. Theseus unwittingly aids this final twist by announcing that it is "almost fairy time." Then, as the mortals leave the stage, Puck replaces them with his superb nocturnal litany and all the fairies troop in to bless the marriages. By coming round to "fairy time" again, the play asserts the validity and constancy of both its worlds, day and night, reason and imagination. By returning from night to day it completes a circle; by reintroducing night it performs a figure eight.

Perhaps the most noticeable fact about time in *A Midsummer Night's Dream* is its minimization. In other Shakespearean plays it has a significant role in the workings of the plot. It untangles the knots of *Twelfth Night,* defeats the lovers in *Romeo and Juliet,* and appears before the curtain to divide *The Winter's Tale* in half. In *A Midsummer Night's Dream,* however, it neither starts nor finishes the action. The events in the woods are a suspension of reality, and their resolution, like their initiation, is extra-temporal. We know that one night has been passed in the woods. But what matters about Bottom's dream (as well as Titania's and the four lovers') is not when it happened or how long it lasted, but that its victim was somehow "translated," was absent from his usual self, another person in another place. In his own thick-witted way, Bottom touches on this when he says that his dream "hath no bottom." He is speaking of it in spatial terms, and such terms seem to be appropriate. Because of the minimization of time in *A Midsummer Night's Dream,* most discussions of its structure tend to emphasize spatial aspects—positioning of character groups, levels of awareness, spheres of action. It is these aspects of the play that we turn to next.

"By some illusion see thou bring her here"   There are two worlds in *A Midsummer Night's Dream*—the kingdom of Theseus and the kingdom of Oberon, the one an orderly society, the other a confusing wilderness. The action of the play moves between the two, as two groups of characters from the real and reasonable world find themselves temporarily lost in the imaginary and irrational world. This pattern of action corresponds closely both to the religious morality and the romance, where

the respective heroes often move on a narrative line that can be schematized as follows:[23]

Morality:

fall from grace / temporary prosperity of evil / divine reconciliation

Romance:

separation / wandering / reunion

As the secular drama came to supersede the religious, it branched out, and one of the variations, based on the pastoral ideal, presented the movement through bad fortune to good fortune in spheres of action already familiar from the romance:

Pastoral Romance:

society / wilderness / an improved society

The purest examples of this pattern in Shakespeare are *As You Like It* and the late romances, *Cymbeline, The Winter's Tale,* and *The Tempest,* but it may be found at work in plays as diverse as *Two Gentlemen* and *King Lear.* In *A Midsummer Night's Dream* it is present at its most comic pitch: the danger which initially sends the central characters into the wilderness is less severe than in, say, *As You Like It,* and the corresponding need for some sort of social reform is slight. The wilderness, as a result, comes to play a more dominant role. In the pastoral romances, it is usually a pseudo-ideal and a temporary haven. In *A Midsummer Night's Dream,* as personified in the fairies, it governs most of the action and controls most of the characters, recalling the more powerful forces of disruption at work in the midsection of both morality and romance.

It will be noted that the spheres of action in these traditional narrative patterns do not alter significantly. It is the characters

23. I owe this schematization to a suggestion in David M. Bevington, *From Mankind to Marlowe* (Cambridge, Mass., 1962), p. 190.

and, by imaginative extension, ourselves who alter as we move through the worlds in question, discovering their interaction. In *A Midsummer Night's Dream,* this process of discovery reveals that the opposing worlds seem to form concentric circles. At first, following the characters from Athens to the woods, we may feel that the two areas are simply adjacent, but as Theseus and daylight reenter the play, we realize that it is possible to enter the woods and reemerge on the other side into human society. Thus, Theseus and his world seem to envelop the world of the woods. But Oberon and Titania, as we learn early in the play and are reminded directly at the end, are not the subjects of Theseus. Their awareness exceeds his, and their world is larger, enveloping his; he is their unconscious subject. Thus we discover another and larger circle, enclosing the first two. Then comes Puck's epilogue, which reminds us that everything we have been watching is a play, an event in a theater with ourselves as audience. Here is a still larger circle, enveloping all the others. The process stops there, but the discovery of ever more comprehensive circles inevitably suggests that there is another one still to be discovered. This is not merely a trick or a display of artistic ingenuity; treating us as it does to an expansion of consciousness and a series of epistemological discoveries, it suggests that our knowledge of the world is less reliable than it seems.

Thus it is that the concentric circles described above can also be used to depict the spectrum of awareness formed by the characters in the play. These are more usually depicted as levels on a kind of rising ladder of intelligence and consciousness,[24] but the very action by which we learn of the differences, that of one character standing aside to watch characters who are less aware of a given situation, suggests the enclosing image of

24. This is the way they are described in an excellent analysis by Bertrand Evans in his *Shakespeare's Comedies* (Oxford, 1960), pp. 33–46.

a circle or sphere. In the inmost circle are the mechanicals, and at their center stands Bottom, supremely ignorant of all that is happening. All of the humor derived from Bottom depends on his absolute lack of awareness joined to the absolute confidence with which he moves through the play. If this makes him amusing, it also makes him sympathetic, as if we unconsciously recognized his kinship not only with the other characters but with ourselves. The difference, after all, is one of degree.

In the next circle belong the lovers; they are not much better off than the clowns, but the fact that they are largely victims of enchantment rather than native stupidity gives them claim to a fuller awareness, since Bottom's enchantment never alters his behavior or his nature. The circle beyond belongs to Theseus and Hippolyta, who oversee the action from a distance and are not victimized by the fairies. Hippolyta deserves the further station, on the basis of her conversation with Theseus at the beginning of the fifth act. The fairies occupy the next circle, Titania first, because she is tricked by her husband, then Oberon and Puck. Even these two, however, are not at all times fully aware of the course of events, and we, the audience, watch them as they watch the others. The furthest circle, then, belongs to us. Or is it the furthest? Does not the playwright belong still further out, overseeing not only the events of the play but our reaction to them, enchanting us as Puck enchants the lovers?

The four groups into which the characters of *A Midsummer Night's Dream* fall present us with another spatial aspect of construction. The effect is like that of a fugue, in which we are simultaneously aware of several lines of movement and thus of position and interaction. Each of the four groups in the play has its own set of experiences. Since we know that these are occurring simultaneously, we are conscious of the location of each group and the ways in which the various actions impinge upon one another. This consciousness is essentially spatial; it requires harmonious resolution just as does the temporal action. If for no other reason, the fairies' entrance in the fifth act would be necessary as the final step in the series of group positionings. The other three groups have gathered there; the arrival of the fairies completes the choreography.

A large part of our interest in the comedy is directed to the way in which the four groups are handled. Their introduction, for example, is formal and at the same time intriguing enough to capture our interest as we gradually realize how the strands of action are to be divided. We meet each group in turn with whatever is necessary in the way of individual and group characterization as well as the details of exposition required to start each action. Theseus and Hippolyta begin the parade with their mood of revelry and a few key details about their wedding. Egeus bustles in, changing the tone and introducing the lovers' plot, with three of the four lovers present. The stage is then cleared for some conventional love dialogue, the plans which will initiate the action in the woods, and the introduction of the fourth lover. In the next scene, we meet the mechanicals and are treated to a full characterization of Bottom. The exposition prepares us for complications in the woods, but it also looks forward, as did that of Theseus, to the final events of the play. For the masque-like introduction of the fairy group, we shift to the second sphere of action. As the last details necessary to the exposition fall into place, Demetrius and Helena enter and the interwoven adventures of three of the groups begin, with Theseus and Hippolyta held in the background for the duration of the night.

It is clear by the time these four groups of characters have been introduced that we are witnessing an art that divides our attention among a number of subjects. The four groups are not unrelated. By the end of the exposition, all have been shown to have the royal wedding as a point of contact: it is the deadline set for Hermia by Theseus, the occasion for the clowns' performance, and the reason for the presence of the fairies. Other linkings and encounters will follow. Nonetheless, each group has a set of common characteristics and each will undergo a particular set of experiences.

The division of interest through multiplication of plots and characters is typical of Elizabethan drama, which has often been called an art of multiplicity.[25] As Madelaine Doran has shown, it originated in medieval practices of narration and staging and continued to be valued in the Renaissance even by those critics who were theoretically committed to the unities.[26] Those dramatists who practiced it risked chaos, since the traditional means of dramatic unification were not open to them. *A Midsummer Night's Dream* risks more than most. Not only does it avoid a single action, it has no central character to whom the various events are unmistakably related. Furthermore, it cannot even be said to have a single theme; its dispersal of interest among various groups and settings is a dispersal, in part, of subject matter as well. Yet Shakespeare achieves unity, partly through careful control of tone and setting and partly through his handling of the groups, a spatial organization which is almost geometrical in its order and which involves relationships within each group as well as among the four.

Our sense of the lovers' permutations, for example, is distinctly spatial; almost any discussion of them is apt to resort to diagrammatic figures.[27] We begin the play with a triangle,

25. Madelaine Doran, *Endeavors of Art* (Madison, Wis., 1954), quotes from Heinrich Wölfflin, *Principles of Art History* (London, 1932), p. 166, and discusses the concept in her first chapter. G. K. Hunter also uses it in his *Lyly*, p. 137 and n. He says the term is used by Rossiter in *English Drama From Early Times to the Elizabethans.* I have not found it there, but Rossiter discusses the concept on pp. 72 f. and in his Epilogue.

26. See Doran, pp. 258–94.

27. The most extensive analysis of this kind is by Baldwin, *Literary Genetics*, pp. 476 f.

Lysander-Hermia-Demetrius, but we soon realize, as Helena's presence and importance is established, that it is in fact a quadrangle, with Helena the neglected corner. In the second act, Lysander's allegiance is suddenly switched, so that we have "cross-wooing," each man pursuing the wrong woman. We also have, as Baldwin points out,[28] a circle, since each of the four parties is pursuing another: Hermia is looking for Lysander; he is wooing Helena; she continues to love Demetrius; and he is still enamored of Hermia. This is the quadrangle at its most disrupted state, and two steps are necessary to repair it. The first of these comes in the third act, when Demetrius is restored to Helena. This reverses the original triangle, and Hermia becomes the neglected party. The fourth act finds the quadrangle in its proper state, each man attached to the right woman, restoring a situation which predates the beginning of the play.

These permutations are further complicated by the question of friendship. Each member of the quadrangle has, potentially, one love and two friends therein, but the shifting of love relationships disrupts the friendships as well. Lysander and Hermia are at the outset alienated from Demetrius but friends of Helena, so much so that they tell her their secret. When Lysander falls in love with Helena, their friendship is of course destroyed; she thinks he is making fun of her. The next alteration, Demetrius' restoration to Helena, destroys the Hermia-Helena friendship: Hermia thinks Helena is somehow responsible; Helena thinks everyone is mocking her. Thus, the restoration of the proper love relationships also restores the friendships of all four; even Lysander and Demetrius, who were ready to fight to the death, are friends again at the end of the play.

The lovers' quadrangle is set within another calmer quadrangle involving the royal couples. We learn of its existence

28. Ibid.

when Oberon and Titania meet. She immediately charges him
with love of Hippolyta, "Your buskin'd mistress and your warrior love," and he counters:

> How canst thou thus, for shame, Titania,
> Glance at my credit with Hippolyta,
> Knowing I know thy love to Theseus?
>
> (II.1.74–76)

There are cross-purposes, it appears, within this group as well.
They do not, however, lead to the complications that beset the
lovers. Theseus and Hippolyta are unaware of the fairies' marital
difficulties. Moreover, the true occasion of the quarrel is the
changeling boy, so that Oberon's practicing on Titania is all that
is needed to restore the quadrangle to harmony and enable the
fairies to join forces for the ritual blessing at the end.

Oberon solves his problems with Titania by finding her an
absurd lover, thus creating a sort of mock triangle with Bottom
as the oblivious third party. But Bottom is also a lover in his role
of Pyramus and is part of another absurd triangle in which he
plays not the intruding beast, lion or ass, but the rightful mate.

These geometrical figures are of course illusory, but by use
of the analogy to which they point, we see more clearly the
constant interaction among the four character groups, the colli-
sions and entanglements which make their separate adventures
interdependent. The lovers begin and end the play with an
attachment to the court of Theseus and the revels surrounding
his wedding. In between, they are the victims of their journey
to the woods and consequent involvement with the fairies. The
fairies, who have arrived to bless the royal wedding, are finally
able to arrange two more and to solve their own difficulties
through an involvement with the mechanicals. The mechanicals, intent on entertaining Theseus, unwittingly entertain
Oberon and Puck as well. Their involvement with the lovers
is more subtle. It is true that their entertainment finally has

the four lovers as audience, but Bottom's adventures, as well
as the play he stars in, provide a good deal of indirect comment
on the lovers, most of it in the form of parody. This kind of
relationship belongs to Shakespeare's practice of "mirroring,"
a spatial technique which deserves a section of its own.

The Wat'ry Glass Shakespeare's device of using scenes, characters, and speeches to point up thematic relationships by means
of reflection has only recently begun to receive critical attention.[29] The term "mirroring" is a useful one, recalling as it does
Hamlet's remarks about art. To say that art mirrors nature is to
suggest more than mere imitation; the process of reflection
sends the image back to its origin and, presumably, stimulates
thought. Ulysses and Achilles discuss the same notion in *Troilus
and Cressida,* using Plato as a springboard. Before Ulysses turns
the idea to Achilles' waning reputation, Achilles himself gives
it a general application:

> For speculation turns not to itself,
> Till it hath travell'd and is mirror'd there
> Where it may see itself. This is not strange at all.
>
> (III.3.109–11)

Mirroring, then, while it may heighten mood and unify action,
can also breed speculation. There is a good deal of evidence to
indicate that Shakespeare used it specifically for "the parallel
advancement of plot and idea."[30]

This function betrays the origins of mirroring; there had been
dramatic devices with the same function and with reasonably

29. Hereward T. Price, "Mirror-Scenes in Shakespeare," in *J. Q.
Adams Memorial Studies* (Washington, D.C., 1948), pp. 101–13;
Reuben A. Brower, *The Fields of Light* (New York, 1951), pp. 95–122;
Maynard Mack, "The Jacobean Shakespeare: Some Observations on the
Construction of the Tragedies," in *Jacobean Theatre,* Stratford-upon-
Avon Studies 1 (New York, 1960), pp. 11–41.

30. Price, p. 103.

similar techniques for some time. The parallel and simultaneous actions of medieval drama sometimes employed reflecting scenes and characters.[31] Medieval drama moves between the realistic and the allegorical so easily and frequently that we are not perhaps inclined to see sequential scenes as mirrors; it would be difficult at times to say which is primary and which reflective. Nonetheless, the fact that these dramas present scenes and characters that are different in kind and thematically alike relates them to the more sophisticated practices which were to follow. After all, *Gorboduc,* which uses allegorical dumb shows to reflect moral and philosophical content, is not very different and not much more sophisticated. Shakespeare's own eventual finesse with the technique in plays like *Lear* and *Hamlet* was the outgrowth of such painful and emblematic beginnings as the fly-killing scene in *Titus* and the dunghill and father–son scenes in the *Henry VI* cycle.

Mirroring in the comedies, less noticed than in the tragedies and histories, has a life and validity of its own. While Shakespeare uses it for the same purposes as in more serious plays, he also employs it concomitantly for comic effect. Perhaps its use as a comic device has distracted attention from its other functions, but mimicry, parody, and exaggeration can mean as much as more serious forms of imitation. The image returned by a funhouse mirror may provoke thought as well as laughter.

We have already noticed the paired characters in *A Midsummer Night's Dream* and noted how they lend symmetry to the plot. Shakespeare also takes advantage of them to set up reflections which underline key dramatic ideas. Thus, the near-identity of the lovers is used to stress the inadequacy of that kind of love which yields itself to irrationality and the conse-

31. See, for instance, the Digby *Mary Magdalene* (in J. Q. Adams, *Chief Pre-Shakespearean Dramas,* pp. 225–42) in which realistic scenes are followed by scenes on separate allegorical stages which mirror the moral crises in the main action.

quent heavy demands upon both personality and intelligence. Demetrius and Lysander address the women they woo in the same conventional vocabulary of exaggerated praise, each mirroring the other's inadequacy. The women expose one another in similar fashion. Hermia has no sooner sworn her love by Cupid's bow and arrow and by "all the vows that ever men have broke" than Helena is on stage for her soliloquy, talking of winged Cupid and Demetrius' broken oaths in the same way. Thus, the two women who think themselves so different—one lucky in love, the other rejected—are shown to have an identity which, incidentally, foreshadows the events to come. Later on, in the woods, Helena herself employs the image of a mirror. Speaking of her earlier desire to be like Hermia, she accounts herself a failure:

> What wicked and dissembling glass of mine,
> Made me compare with Hermia's sphery eyne?
> (II.2.98–99)

It is at precisely this moment that Lysander wakes up and falls in love with her. "Transparent Helena," he shouts, not seeing in her the image of his folly. He too goes on to insist that she and Hermia are completely different. Throughout the night, the four lovers will peer at each other and always fail to see what the playwright makes so clear to us, their likenesses.

Much the same thing can be said about the royal pairs. It is appropriate that Theseus, as representative of daylight and right reason, should have subdued his bride-to-be to the rule of his masculine will. That is the natural order of things.[32] It is equally appropriate that Oberon, as king of darkness and fantasy, should have lost control of his wife, and that the corresponding natural

---

32. This point is extensively discussed in Olson, "*A Midsummer Night's Dream* and the Meaning of Court Marriage," pp. 101 ff. He cites the Theseus of *The Two Noble Kinsmen* as a more explicit example.

disorder described by Titania should ensue. All the details in these dual situations have the same function. Both royal pairs love panoramas, but the landscapes they see are appropriately different. The means that each king employs to establish rule in his kingdom are significantly opposed. Even the Masters of the Revels of each monarchy, Philostrate and Puck, serve to strengthen the sense of contrast within likeness.

What we have here differs from the mirroring found in the tragedies. There, the tragic hero occupies the center of attention, while surrounding characters reflect him, as Horatio, Laertes, and Fortinbras mirror Hamlet, or while alternate scenes reflect his dilemma, as do the Gloucester scenes in *Lear*. In these plays, mirroring works mostly one way. Even the standard mirror device found in earlier comedies, the servant subplot, has this characteristic. Since *A Midsummer Night's Dream* cannot be said to have a central character, however, or even a central group of characters, any mirroring that takes place is necessarily reflexive or retroactive, throwing as much meaning on one scene, group, or character as on another. This is another illustration of the way in which diffusion marks this play, as well, I believe, as other Shakespearean comedies, where mirroring has the same two-way effect. If we could accept this, we would stop speaking of plot and subplot in Shakespearean comedy and recognize the uniqueness of its form. Nor need we be afraid of admitting to disunity. The continually rebounding reflections constantly strengthen identity, suggesting that everything we see is an aspect of the same situation and bringing to the play a startlingly organic unity. Again I think it accurate to stress the germinal role of *A Midsummer Night's Dream* in the development of this technique; while there are hints of it in *Love's Labour's Lost,* it was not until *A Midsummer Night's Dream* that Shakespeare found the means to use it fully.

If any group of characters in the play may be said to exist primarily for purposes of reflection, it is the mechanicals. This does not subordinate them in importance; they could easily claim supreme position as the busiest glasses in this comedy of reflection. What is more, they bring to the climax of the play its biggest and funniest mirror. Their reflective function is worth examining in some detail.

The mechanicals' first scene gives us hints of the echo and parody we are to have from them through the rest of the play. Their concern for an orderly handling of their task catches the theme Theseus has just sounded and will continue to sound throughout the play. Their respect for hierarchy recalls the issue raised by the entrance of Egeus and the lovers,[33] and their plans for rehearsal echo the plans of Demetrius and Hermia. Their confused use of language (e.g. "I will aggravate my voice") presents an aspect of the confusion that will later reign in the woods, and the paradoxes they blunder into, "lamentable comedy," "monstrous little voice," hint at the doubts about familiar categories—dreaming and waking, reason and imagination—with which the play will eventually leave us. The interlude about true love they plan to perform promises to mock the lovers we have just seen. Finally, Bottom's enthusiastic confidence that he can perform any role—tyrant, lover, maiden, or lion—amusingly introduces us to the theme of metamorphosis, the activity which will dominate all experience in the woods.

All of these echoes, or pre-echoes, it should be added, are those that remain within the context of the play's events. Others, directed at the knowing audience, have already begun to parody such "outside" targets as bad plays, whining poetry, and court fashion. These mirrorings prepare the audience for the subtler parodies involved in the lovers' plot and dialogue, bring it into a closer relationship with the play, and open the way for some

33. "These common life characters . . . furnish a rule of ignorant common sense against which the vagaries of their superiors may be measured. So the first act closes by showing the persistence of order in the lower segment of society" (Ibid., p. 106).

of the insights into the nature of dramatic illusion which the play ultimately provides.

Once in the woods, the clowns keep up a continuous comic counterpoint to the adventures of the lovers. When Hermia rushes off in search of errant Lysander ("Either death or you I'll find immediately"), the cast of "Pyramus and Thisby" troops on ("Are we all met?") to rehearse another story of desperate love. By virtue of its versification, their language is more mechanical than what we have just heard from Lysander and will soon hear from Demetrius, but the vocabulary and tone are similar. Like Lysander and Demetrius, Bottom, playing the role of a faithful lover, finds himself the victim of a sudden transformation. The other clowns flee, but Bottom as Ass stays on to become the paramour of the fairy queen. Their beauty and beast tableaux alternate with the comings and goings of the lovers, each reflecting the absurdity of the other.

Verbal echoes strengthen the mirror relationships. Lysander swears to Helena that reason brings him to her:

> The will of man is by his reason sway'd;
> And reason says you are the worthier maid.
> Things growing are not ripe until their season;
> So I, being young, till now not ripe to reason;
> And touching now the point of human skill,
> Reason becomes the marshal to my will
> And leads me to your eyes.
>
> (II.2.115–21)

Bottom echoes him more sensibly when Titania first admits that she has fallen in love at first sight:

> Methinks, mistress, you should have little reason for that. And yet, to say the truth, reason and love keep little company together now-a-days. The more the pity that some honest neighbours will not make them friends.
>
> (III.1.145–50)

Demetrius, once in the woods, thinks his problem is to find Hermia:

> Thou told'st me they were stol'n unto this wood;
> And here am I, and wood within this wood
> Because I cannot greet my Hermia.
>
> (II.1.191–93)

The problem, as Bottom suggests, is much simpler than that:

> if I had wit enough to get out of this wood, I have enough to serve mine own turn.
>
> (III.1.153–54)

Stupid as he may be, Bottom is not the victim of love's madness and so, throughout the night of errors, conducts himself with greater dignity and common sense. The distortive mirror can also serve as a corrective.

As object of Titania's affection, Bottom mirrors not only the Athenians, but the fairy queen's earlier loves as well. He is a kind of mock-Oberon, a role he tries valiantly to play, sending the fairies off on appropriate errands just as Oberon has sent Puck for the little Western flower, but of course his asshood keeps betraying him into unkingly needs:

> Methinks I have a great desire to a bottle of hay.
> Good hay, sweet hay, hath no fellow.
>
> (IV.1.35–36)

Titania has also been, and will again be, in love with Theseus, and she has led him, as she leads Bottom, through "the glimmering night." Theseus has put such experiences behind him. He would probably agree with Quince that "A paramour is (God bless us!) a thing of naught" (IV.2.13–14). But Bottom's adventures offer a farcical reminder of events in Theseus' past. Thus, a clown's dream becomes one of the key mirrors in the play, reflecting almost all of the male characters in one way or another. Bottom is not the succeful actor he had hoped to be, but he gets his chance to play a number of roles—not just lover and tyrant, but several kinds of lover and one or two kinds of tyrant; not lion, but a beast at least as interesting if not nearly as frightening.

"Pyramus and Thisby" is the climax of the mechanicals' reflective career. If it does not succeed in holding the mirror up to nature, it holds it up to almost everything else. "The best in this kind are but shadows," says Theseus. Shadows of what? Of the events and characters of *A Midsummer Night's Dream*, but the audience of "Pyramus and Thisby" may be partially pardoned for not recognizing their own images. The lovers, back from the woods and safely married, need not compare their experiences with those of Pyramus and Thisby in a less accommodating wood. Nor can they be expected so soon to recognize in the poetry of the play the inadequate language of their own vocabulary of love. Theseus and Hippolyta, too, have put their pasts behind them; nothing about this play is able to provoke their memories. The mechanicals, as with the other effects of the drama, fail in this function too; "speculation turns not to itself."

Not, that is, among the characters of the play. But we are also the audience of "Pyramus and Thisby" and have many comparisons to make. The resemblance between the "fond pageant" in the woods and the "tragical mirth" in the palace does not escape us, nor do the references to at least some of the other plays and the various dramatic and poetic conventions which the playwright finds hard to admire. Beyond these reflections we begin to discern an even larger one. Perhaps it is begun by Theseus' remarks about the poet, but it is the kind of insight that ought to be provoked by any play within a play, a mirror for the audience–drama relationship if ever there was one. Shakespeare exploits it thoroughly. Within a play about love written for a wedding, he puts a play about love written for a wedding. If

"Pyramus and Thisby" is inept, it is also well-meaning and deserving of charity; so is *A Midsummer Night's Dream*. If Bottom and his fellows can expect sixpence a day for life as their reward, so perhaps does Shakespeare's company deserve generous remuneration. But there are contrasts too. Where the mechanicals fail at dramatic illusion, unity, and appropriateness, *A Midsummer Night's Dream* succeeds. The playwright manages to exploit the contrast as a kind of mild reminder that he knows his business; he can even afford to parody himself (assuming that this play follows *Romeo and Juliet*). This is perhaps what gave Max Beerbohm the impression that in this play, "we have the Master, confident in his art, at ease with it as a man in his dressing-gown, kicking up a loose slipper and catching it on his toe."[34]

The discerning audience will finally find in the mirror of the mechanicals' performance one more image—its own. They are bound to notice that "Pyramus and Thisby" does not have a very perceptive audience. Not that it deserves one, but as *A Midsummer Night's Dream* is superior to "Pyramus and Thisby," so, the playwright seems to hope, will its audience be superior. Elizabethan audiences, we know, were not always as attentive or polite as the actors and playwrights might wish. Pehaps they were being asked in this comedy, as well as in *Love's Labour's Lost,* to recognize their image and reform it altogether. Certainly they are given a chance to behave more astutely than the audience of "Pyramus and Thisby," to see to it that they are not quite as condescending as Theseus, as inconsistent as Hippolyta, as oblivious, when faced with their own images, as the lovers. The playwright, by placing them higher than any of the characters in the play, gives them every opportunity. If they should fail, they have only themselves to blame. There is just a hint of mockery in Puck's epilogue:

34. Quoted in the New Cambridge Edition, p. xix.

> If we shadows have offended,
> Thinke but this, and all is mended—
> That you have but slumb'red here
> While these visions did appear.
> And this weak and idle theme,
> No more yielding but a dream.
>   (V.1.430–35)

Anyone who is willing to admit that he has slept through this performance cannot claim to be very alert. In fact, he must inevitably be compared to those characters in the play who are willing to think that they have "dreamed" it, dismissing events which exposed them significantly. Shakespeare gives us our choice. We may remain within the outer circles of consciousness with Oberon, Puck, and himself, or we may doze off and fall inward toward the condition of Bottom and the lovers. In the mirror of *A Midsummer Night's Dream,* the spectator may find, even if he does not recognize, his very form and pressure.

If we now draw back to summarize the various stylistic and structural devices exhibited in the preceding pages, we will begin to discover how closely they are related, how much a part of a single, overarching artistic purpose. The multiplicity of this drama, its division of interest, is revealed in its characterizations and groupings, in the exposition and careful counterpointing of the several plots, in the diversity of styles which support all this diffusion, and in those stylistic and structural devices which emphasize spaciousness and abundance. But Shakespeare's is an art that divides to reunite. The multiple activities and beings we see belong to a single panorama. The devices that bring them together range from the schematized relationships of the plot to the extremely subtle interplay of reflections in language and action. The sharing of likenesses among the most diverse and unlikely elements of the play serves to unite them even as it functions to surprise and amuse us. Finally, when it has accomplished its miraculous union of materials, the play calls attention to itself as an artistic entity, inviting us to muse, as we return to reality, on the nature and significance of illusion. This last touch, expressed with humility, has behind it a certain bravado, the confidence of a master artist. It is almost as though a magician had revealed the deceptions on which his art depended, confident that our credulity would put us back in his hands when it came time for the next trick. This is to suggest not that Shakespeare thought his art false or misleading, but that he was strongly aware of its techniques and effects at this point and equally conscious of the discrepancy between his own knowledge and that of his audience.

What, finally, may be said of the relation of *A Midsummer Night's Dream* to the development of Shakespeare's dramaturgy? Facile comparisons are impossible. Shakespeare was not an artist to repeat himself, so we do not discover startling parallels of character and situation between this play and later ones. To demonstrate the exact position of *A Midsummer Night's Dream* in Shakespeare's development would require an exhaustive comparison both of earlier and later plays which is not possible here. My method must be to claim little but hopefully suggest much. I will content myself with two specific observations. First, as indicated above, I believe that Shakespeare developed a comedy of multiple interest in which he achieved organic unity not by subordination of one element to another (as continued to be partly the case in his tragedies) but by a careful thematic control through which diverse elements were shown to be facets of the same idea. He developed this kind of comedy from Lyly's comedies of debate, gradually shifting the emphasis from debate to action and character.[35] *Love's Labour's*

35. It is to Hunter's discussion of Lyly's structuring techniques that I owe the idea of unification around a debate topic.

Lost is his first try, and the unification by debate is still very prominent. In *A Midsummer Night's Dream,* however, in which I maintain that he first mastered the form to his own satisfaction, the debate subjects have receded into the background. They are still there for those who wish to discern them—daylight and reason versus moonlight and imagination—but they are expressed through character and event rather than by argument. I think that it could be shown that later comedies—including the late romances—employ this same structure and are most profitably analyzed in this light. It should be noted, moreover, that Shakespeare's use of the technique is not strictly limited to his comic practice. Whenever he had diverse elements to unify, he was apt to resort not to unity of time, place, or event, but to unity of idea, achieved by the devices that first came to full fruition in *A Midsummer Night's Dream.*

The second point has to do with the relation of plot to poetry and of structure, to use the terms of this chapter, to style. It is generally said or implied in discussions of Shakespeare's development that he began with an imperfect union of these two aspects of his art and gradually learned to integrate them. Just when he mastered the problem is not a matter of general agreement. Many critics have professed to see in *A Midsummer Night's Dream* the disjunction of style and structure characteristic of Shakespeare's earliest work. If this chapter has achieved its purpose, it has shown that the poetry of this play is completely wedded to the needs and demands of the multiple plot. In fact, this discussion has imposed a division which does not really exist. The moments of stylistic bravura, we have seen, are an integral part of the play's structure, and the constant use of mirroring is just as much a stylistic device as a technique for achieving unity of form. *A Midsummer Night's Dream,* then, can be seen as a solution to the playwright's problem of uniting poetry and plot, one of the earliest in his canon.

3 ✳ Bottom's Dream

Those which have compared our life unto a dreame, have happily had more reason so to doe, then they were aware. When we dreame, our soule liveth, worketh and excerciseth all her faculties, even, and as much, as when it waketh; and if more softly and obscurely, yet verily not so, as that it may admit so great a difference, as there is between a darke night and a cleare day: Yea as betweene a night and a shadow: There it sleepeth, here it slumbreth: More or lesse, they are ever darknesses, yea Cimmerian darknesses. We wake sleeping and sleep waking.

MONTAIGNE

There is no Arte delivered to mankinde that hath not the workes of Nature for his principall object, without which they could not consist, and on which they so depend, as they become Actors and Players, as it were, of what Nature will have set foorth.

SIDNEY

AN IS BUT AN ASS," SAYS BOTTOM, "IF he go about to expound this dream." That might serve as a warning to commentators. Serious discussions of comedy always take place near the precipice of academic fatuity. Nonetheless, it is possible to be too cautious; studies of Shakespeare's philosophical and psychological preoccupations have in the past dealt almost exclusively with the tragedies and histories. Such exclusion inevitably leaves the impression that the comedies are somehow thoughtless. More recently, plays like *Troilus and Cressida* have been shown to have serious content, but such content, it is usually suggested, exists at the expense of comic potential. *Troilus* is rich in ideas, at least as rich as *Hamlet,* but it is not very funny, and these two facts are often treated as if they illustrated some inexorable aesthetic law. Thus, the funnier comedies are still widely felt to be trivial in content, and a comparison between, say, *As You Like It* and *Lear* would strike most people as unprofitable and even absurd.

A Midsummer Night's Dream has suffered seriously from the charge of intellectual triviality. Those who dislike the play always attack it upon these grounds. Samuel Pepys stated their case succinctly:

1662, September 29:—To the King's Theatre, where we saw "Midsummer Night's Dream," which I had never seen before, nor shall ever again, for it is the most insipid, ridiculous play, that ever I saw in my life.[1]

Those who simply tolerate the play leave the same impression. An eighteenth-century editor called it "one of the wild and irregular Overflowings of this great Author's creative Imagination."[2] This suggests that the play has interest, but sharply defines its limitations.

It is the admirers of *Dream,* however, who have in the past probably done it the greatest disservice, for they have found nothing to praise but its lightness, innocence, and fanciful gaiety; these qualities, by themselves, suggest brainlessness. Until recently, discussions of the play usually stressed grace, lyricism, and form and were unfortunately noticeable for the liberal use of adjectives like "gossamer" and "silken." Moreover, friends of the play would not have their darling violated by heavy-footed analysis. Witness the watchdog stance of J. O. Halliwell-Phillips:

> What is absurdly termed aesthetic criticism is more out of place on this comedy than on any other of Shakespeare's plays. It deadens the "native woodnotes wild" that every reader of taste would desire to be left to their own influences. The *Midsummer Night's Dream* is too exquisite a composition to be dulled by the infliction of philosophical analysis.[3]

1. Samuel Pepys, *Diary,* ed. Henry B. Wheatley (10 vols. London, 1928–35), 5, 347. Pepys probably saw a fairly intact version of the play. What impressed him most, however, was "some good dancing and some handsome women."

2. Anonymous, *The Companion to the Play-House* or An Historical Account of all the Dramatick Writers (and their Works) that have appeared in Great Britain and Ireland. FROM THE Commencement of our Theatrical Exhibitions down to the Present Year, 1764. London, 1764.

3. J. O. Halliwell-Phillips, *Memoranda on the Midsummer Night's Dream* (Brighton, 1879), p. 13.

Surely we have come to find more in this play than "native wood-notes wild" and the limitations they imply. Surely, too, we can begin to hope for productions of the play which do not treat it as a kind of Elizabethan *Peter Pan.* The stock reaction to fairies and magic is apt to be a childish one, but as we have begun to get over that in connection with *The Tempest,* so may we hope to do with *A Midsummer Night's Dream.*

I do not wish to present myself as a lone champion, rescuing an important play from neglect and misclassification. The trend of thought I have described has been for some time in the process of correction. Frank Kermode's suggestion that the play is Shakespeare's best comedy is less astounding today than it would have been twenty years ago.[4] The trilogy of "especially mythological plays in which Shakespeare is working intensively at the instrument of thought" discussed by Elizabeth Sewell[5] links the *Dream* with *Lear* and *The Tempest* in an especially illuminating way. With these and other encouragements, and with what I hope is the proper amount of caution, I go about to expound this dream.

My contention in this chapter is that the richness of interest of *A Midsummer Night's Dream* lies, in large part, in its expression of contemporaneous intellectual issues, issues which frequently take the form of oppositions. Some of these were of particular interest to the artist, more specifically to the Elizabethan playwright, but most were engaging all the thoughtful men of the late Renaissance. The problem of Shakespeare's specific intention, the degree of deliberation with which he approached these ideas, seems to me both insoluble and unprofitable, and I have sought to avoid it here by pointing out ideas which are indubitably present in the play and showing the ways in which they are analogous to the ideas which pre-

4. Frank Kermode, "The Mature Comedies" in *Early Shakespeare,* Stratford-upon-Avon Studies 3 (New York, 1961), p. 214.

5. Sewell, *The Orphic Voice,* p. 155.

occupied Shakespeare's contemporaries. The reader may draw his own conclusions about how they got there. My own view, for that matter, holds that poetry is a form of thought, that it asks and tries to answer great questions, and that it is therefore not surprising that the work of a great artist, whether heavy tragedy or light comedy, should be found as rich and complex in its handling of ideas as the work of any other thinker.

This chapter explores a technique of dramatic expression which should be explained at the outset, since it links the techniques of comedy with the possibility of intellectual content. In terms of comic method, it is the familiar process of reversal, the use of opposites to create amusement. If we recall any basic comic situation, we see how it works: dignity is subjected to indignity; the master is governed by the servant; stupidity triumphs over intelligence; and so forth. The comic vision is relative and skeptical. It insists that if one thing is true, its opposite may just as well be true, and it finds thousands of ways to demonstrate this. The Elizabethans were familiar with the technique and had at least two terms for it—"misrule" and "handy-dandy." Both words apply to the principle of reversal as an accepted process on a wide scale, and misrule, at least, suggests functions for it other than amusement.

If we apply the notion of reversal, or misrule, to the handling of ideas, we see how the artist can use it to force us into a temporary relativity of judgment and belief. He can balance opposing values and forces in a way that allows us to commit ourselves wholeheartedly to neither. Insofar as he is consistently comic, he will maintain this balance in every direction, reserving reconciliation and commitment for the ending. For the duration of the work, reason as a value will exist on equal terms with unreason as a value, order with disorder, and so forth. Moreover, it seems clear that the comic artist does not maintain his balances reluctantly, but from a conviction of their accuracy and rightness. Prejudice, dogmatism, any excessive confidence in point of view are his natural targets, and the process of handy-dandy is his weapon. While this is hardly a complete account of the comic viewpoint, it will serve as an introduction to what seems to me an important Shakespearean working principle. Throughout *A Midsummer Night's Dream*, conventional Elizabethan dichotomies are presented in a way which undermines the assurance with which they were constructed and used by orthodox thinkers. The process, as I have suggested, is perfectly compatible with the comic mode.

"A most rare vision"   The Elizabethan sense of "dream" is close to our own, although more pejorative, since the Elizabethans attached little value to the subconscious. Serious thinkers regarded the interpretation of dreams as a kind of superstition. Most dreams had purely physiological causes and could thus, as Bacon suggests, be easily explained:

> The interpretation of natural dreams has been much labored; but mixed with numerous extravagancies. We shall here only observe of it, that at present it stands not upon its best foundation; which, that where the same thing happens from an internal cause, as also happens from an external one, there the external action passes into a dream. Thus the stomach may be oppressed by a gross internal vapor, as well as by an external weight; whence those who have the nightmare dream that a weight is laid upon them, with a great concurrence of circumstances.
>
> (*Advancement of Learning,* Bk. IV, Chap. 1)[6]

In sleep, as Burton points out, the outward senses are closed off and "the phantasy alone is free,"[7] leaving the mind no con-

6. Sir Francis Bacon, *Advancement of Learning and Novum Organum,* ed. J. E. Creighton (London, 1900), pp. 108–09.

7. Robert Burton, *The Anatomy of Melancholy* (Philadelphia, 1869), p. 103.

tact with reality. Thus, although the possibility of divine com-
munication was always held out, dream experience was largely
regarded as illusory. As Nashe put it:

> A dreame is nothing els but a bubling scum or froath of
> the fancie, which the day hath left undigested; or an after
> feast made of the fragments of idle imaginations.[8]

By analogy, any insubstantial and deceptive experience could
be called a dream. The usage was derogatory. Shakespeare himself resorted to it frequently in just this sense. Tarquin admits
to himself that the rape he is contemplating will be "a dream,
a breath, a froth of fleeting joy" (*Lucrece*, 212). Margaret reminds Elizabeth that she is a "poor shadow, painted queen. . . .
A dream of what thou wert, a breathe, a bubble" (*Richard III*,
IV.4.83–88). Flavius notes that Timon has lived "in a dream of
friendship" (*Timon*, IV.2.34). These uses of the word reflect
the sensible contemporary attitude, summed up in Mercutio's
definition:

> I talk of dreams;
> Which are the children of an idle brain,
> Begot of nothing but vain fantasy;
> Which is as thin of substance as the air,
> And more inconstant than the wind.
> (*Romeo*, I.4.96–100)

Corollary to the concept of dream as illusory experience is
the idea that any knowledge connected with dreams is false and
misleading. This is precisely Mercutio's point; he is warning
Romeo not to trust the premonitions he has had in his dream.

8. Thomas Nashe, "The Terrors of the Night," *Works*, ed. R. B.
McKerrow, rev. F. P. Wilson (5 vols. Oxford, 1958), *1*, 355.

Again, by extension, any false knowledge could be called a dream, and any transition from misunderstanding to understanding, from delusion to truth, could be compared to the process of awakening. "Learn, good soul," says Richard to his queen:

> To think our former state a happy dream;
> From which awak'd, the truth of what we are
> Shows us but this.
>> (*Richard II,* V.1.17–20)

Life itself, by extension, could be criticized as a dream. Chapman reflects the contemporary fondness for the image:

> Man is a torch borne in the wind, a dream
> But of a shadow, summ'd with all his substance.
>> (*Bussy d'Ambois,* I.1.19–20)

Prospero finds man and his life as insubstantial as dreams, and the "fantastical Duke of dark corners" seconds him:

> Thou hast nor youth nor age,
> But as it were an after-dinner's sleep,
> Dreaming on both.
>> (*Measure for Measure,* III.1.32–34)

The reader will note in these references to dreams a cluster of images—shadow, wind, breath, bubble, froth, torch—which were conventionally invoked to express the insubstantiality of dreams and dreamlike experience. To this group we may add "player" and "stage." The interesting but deceptive knowledge and experience of dreams were inevitably compared to the character and content of art by its detractors and, occasionally, by its defenders and practitioners as well. Images from the theater became synonyms for the unreal. Stephen Gosson could express his contempt for actors by pointing out that their battles, for instance, were merely occasions "to encounter a shadow, or conquere a paper monster."[9] Francis Bacon could give poetry what he thought was its due by calling it

> a thing sweet and varied, and that would be thought to have in it something divine; a character which dreams likewise affect. But now it is time for me to awake, and rising above the earth to wing my way through the clear air of Philosophy and the Sciences.
>
> (*Advancement of Learning,* Bk. III, Chap. 1)[10]

The phrase "clear air" strengthens the metaphor, suggesting that poetry and dreams are inevitably grounded in a sort of murky night of the understanding. "Shadow," as used in connection with dreams, connoted obscurity as well as impalpability.

The artists themselves, in gestures of modesty and humility, were apt to emphasize the trivial and insubstantial nature of their work, often in order to escape serious criticism. Sidney's uneasy defense of poetry suggests that poets do not lie because they do not affirm anything. The distinction moves crucially close to the shadow–substance polarity. Lyly could thus protect himself by comparing his art to dreaming. In the prologue to *The Woman in the Moon,* he argues that the play is merely the product of his slumber, asking:

> If many faults escape in her discourse,
> Remember all is but a Poets dreame.[11]

9. Stephen Gosson, *The School of Abuse,* Shakespeare Society Reprints (London, 1841), p. 11.

10. Quoted and discussed in Sewell, *The Orphic Voice,* p. 75. The translation is Spedding's.

11. Lyly, *Works, 3,* 241.

In the prologue to *Sapho and Phao,* he turns the idea toward the audience, entreating the queen:

> that your Highnesse imagine your self to be in a deepe dreame, that staying the conclusion, in your rising your Majestie vouchsafe but to saye, *And so you awakte.*[12]

Shakespeare, by titling his play a dream, resorts to the same convention, even if he is not willing to treat it as simply.

There was very little that was positive to balance against the widespread attitude toward dreams as illusory knowledge and experience. It was still considered possible, if not likely, that divine agency might make use of dreams to convey information or inspiration to human beings. Burton, recalling medieval practice, lists several kinds of dreams—"naturall, divine, demoniacall, &c."—but his interest in their possible value is half-hearted. He suggests that they vary "according to humours, diet, actions, objects, &c" and offers advice on how to avoid them.[13] His attitude reflects a low ebb of scientific and philosophical interest in dreams.

In literary circles, however, some attention was still paid to the medieval literary form of the dream allegory or vision. Since we know that Shakespeare drew upon Chaucer's *Legend of Good Women* in *A Midsummer Night's Dream,* we can be sure that he was familiar with the dream vision as a device. His use of dream must therefore be linked to Chaucerian practice, suggesting a literary heritage in which the dream was a respectable source of knowledge, even when it was merely a means for introducing fantasy and allegory. Lyly had already made some use of the tradition; he introduced dreams within his plays which served either to convey allegorical information or to intensify thematic meaning. Endymion's long and emblematic

12. Ibid., 2, 372.
13. Burton, *Anatomy of Melancholy,* pp. 103, 326.

dream does both.[14] The same practice is represented in Shakespeare by Hermia's experience in the second act:

> Help me, Lysander, help me! Do thy best
> To pluck this crawling serpent from my breast!
> Aye me, for pity! What a dream was here!
> Lysander, look how I do quake with fear.
> Methought a serpent eat my heart away,
> And you sat smiling at his cruel prey.
> Lysander! What, remov'd?
>
> (II.2.145–51)

Hermia's dream, as the audience realizes, is an accurate, if symbolic, account of what has just happened and is therefore not just a dream in the sense that Hermia hopes it is. As one example of a "true" dream, it joins the complex system of dream experiences that constitutes the play.

Shakespeare's characteristic practice with something like the dreaming–waking polarity is to question both concepts, turning them against each other until they acquire a paradoxical relationship. Sometimes a single character is involved, like Christopher Sly, whose dilemma we enjoy because he is, in fact, both awake and dreaming:

> Am I a lord? and have I such a lady?
> Or do I dream? or have I dream'd till now?
> (*Shrew,* Ind.2.70–71)

More often the dreaming–waking confusion involves several characters and large portions of dramatic action. Perdita, after Polixenes has condemned her, draws the familiar contrast:

14. Lyly, *Works, 3,* 66–67. See also Hunter's discussion of this dream in his *Lyly,* pp. 185 f.

Of your own state take care. This dream of mine—
Being now awake, I'll queen it no inch farther.
(*Winter's Tale,* IV.4.459–60)

What the audience knows, however, is the secret of Perdita's
royalty. She does have a right to "queen it," and her waking
state, which she thinks real, is more deceptive than her dream.
The same kind of irony is illustrated in Mercutio's chiding of
Romeo, cited above. For all his common sense, he is wrong,
and Romeo is right to suspect that his foreboding dream has
validity. Prince Hal's repudiation of Falstaff raises the same
question:

How ill white hairs become a fool and jester!
I have long dreamt of such a kind of man,
So surfeit-swell'd, so old, and so profane;
But being awak'd, I do despise my dream.
(*2 Henry IV,* V.5.52–55)

Hal's metaphor is convenient to the moment, but not entirely
convincing. We are not sure that his experience of Falstaff can
be dismissed as a dream, and we wonder whether his waking
state will be, as he suggests, superior.

There can be no doubt of Cleopatra's intention when, after
Antony's death, she sets out to defend dreams:

You laugh when boys or women tell their dreams;
Is't not your trick?
Dol.   I understand not, madam.
Cleo. I dreamt there was an Emperor Antony—
O, such another sleep, that I might see
But such another man!
(*Antony and Cleopatra,* V.2.74–78)

With Antony dead, Caesar's world has become real and Antony's a dream, but there is still no comparison between the two. Not only can Antony not be dismissed, he is, paradoxically, having vanished, superior to what remains and is real. After her famous speech on Antony's size and greatness, Cleopatra asks:

> Think you there was or might be such a man
> As this I dreamt of?
> *Dol.*   Gentle madam, no.
> *Cleo.* You lie, up to the hearing of the gods!
> But, if there be or ever were one such,
> It's past the size of dreaming. Nature wants stuff
> To vie strange forms with fancy; yet, t'imagine
> An Antony were nature's piece 'gainst fancy,
> Condemning shadows quite.
>
> (V.2.93–100)

All the conventional distinctions between fact and fantasy, shadow and substance, dreaming and waking, and art and nature are broken down here to make room in the historical imagination for Antony's greatness, exaggerated and insubstantial, but somehow more real than the living Caesar and all his imperial pretense. Cleopatra joins the long list of Shakespearean characters who lose their confidence in the easy dichotomies of the reasonable and practical world. For her, as for others, the concept of the dream as delusion undergoes ironic reversal.

The process of reversal is used throughout *A Midsummer Night's Dream* in connection with the dreaming–waking opposition. Most of the characters have an experience which they find difficult to classify except as dream, a means of dismissing it as unreal. Hermia's serpent dream, cited above, is the only example of an actual dream in the play, but it is merely the first in a series of experiences which are described as dreams. Titania is waked from sleep by Bottom, but she wakes into a dreamlike state in which she is decidedly not herself. She later calls her experience a "vision," suggesting that she has been asleep. When Bottom is pointed out to her, she recognizes that her dream has actually occurred.

The same cannot be said of the lovers. Oberon predicts correctly when he says:

> When they next wake, all this derision
> Shall seem a dream and fruitless vision.
>
> (III.2.370–71)

Human knowledge is not equal to fairy knowledge, and it is not long before the lovers are ready to classify their adventures in the woods as dreams. Demetrius expresses a momentary doubt, but it is quickly resolved:

> Are you sure
> That we are awake? It seems to me
> That yet we sleep, we dream. Do not you think
> The Duke was here, and bid us follow him?
>
> *Her.* Yea, and my father.
> *Hel.*   And Hippolyta.
> *Lys.* And he did bid us follow to the temple.
> *Dem.* Why then, we are awake. Let's follow him,
> And by the way let us recount our dreams.
>
> (IV.1.195–202)

When the dreams turn out to be remarkably similar, only Hippolyta wonders at the fact. Theseus expresses the common-sense attitude: what happened to the lovers is outside the realm of ordinary experience and explanation; therefore, it must be unreal, the insubstantial product of their dreaming fantasies.

It is Bottom who wakes up last. It is characteristic of the paradoxical atmosphere of the play that he should show the most respect for dreams and, as the stupidest character, come closest to the truth. Even if his dream is only a dream, it is far more important than ordinary experience:

> I have had a most rare vision. I have had a dream, past the wit of man to say what dream it was. Man is but an ass if he go about to expound this dream. Methought I was—there is no man can tell what. Methought I was, and methought I had.—But man is but a patch'd fool, if he will offer to say what methought I had. The eye of man hath not heard, the ear of man hath not seen, man's hand is not able to taste, his tongue to conceive, nor his heart to report, what my dream was.
>
> (IV.1.203 ff.)

Here, where "dream" and "rare vision" are equated and the suggestion of an encounter with divinity is strengthened by a comically scrambled passage from the Bible, we are closer, amid our laughter, to the mystery of dream experience than at any other point in the play. Bottom's awe at this vision "past the wit of man" is enormously suggestive in terms of our normal contempt for the shadowy, irrational world of dreams, for, all things considered, he is right, and his healthy respect for his limitations gives him a more accurate sense of what has passed than is possessed either by the lovers or by Theseus. It is also significant that in his wordless confusion, in his discovery that his dream is not reportable by normal means, Bottom's instinct is to have it turned into art:

> I will get Peter Quince to write a ballet of this dream. It shall be call'd "Bottom's Dream," because it hath no bottom; and I will sing it in the latter end of our play, before the Duke.
>
> (IV.1.218–22)

The ballad is never performed, but the concept of the work of art as dream is picked up again in Puck's epilogue:

> If we shadows have offended,
> Think but this, and all is mended—
> That you have but slumb'red here
> While these visions did appear.
> And this weak and idle theme,
> No more yielding but a dream.
>
> (V.1.430–35)

If this were the only such reference in the play, it might be correct to take it as the conventional flourish of apology, making use of the commonplace metaphor of dream as false and trivial experience. But in the light of all the other events in the play, the statement cannot be read as serious, straightforward, or without irony. If we are willing to say that the play is a dream and, as a result, inconsequential, then we are no better than the characters we have just been laughing at. If we have learned anything from the play, we have learned to be wary of dismissing unusual experiences as meaningless dreams and of regarding dreams as yielding no significant knowledge. Puck's invitation must be heard or read in the light of these perceptions. It then becomes one more blow at the customary distinction between dream experience and waking experience.

Why does Shakespeare, at the last moment, choose to connect his art to the concept he has been turning over within the play? We have seen that the theatrical images had joined the group commonly associated with unreality and false knowledge. Thus, there is nothing unusual in the connection. As presented, it offers a lighthearted and glancing challenge to those who criticized the theater as a place where shadows acted out insubstantial and meaningless fancies and to serious thinkers who dismissed poetic knowledge as misleading and meaningless, "a dream of learning." Shakespeare's strategy is not to contradict these strictures, but to accept them, at first apparently on their own terms, but ultimately in order to show that those terms are meaningless. This is not to insist that Shakespeare believed in dreams or divinations or, for that matter, fairies. It is to suggest that he found them already in use as metaphors and turned them to his own purposes in order to express a comical and skeptical vision of human experience and to defend, not so much by assertion as by demonstration, the value of his art.

"The gatherings of the senses"   Reason and imagination were often set in opposition by Renaissance thinkers, but, like dreaming and waking, shadow and substance, they were not considered equals. Imagination might sometimes get the upper hand in dreams or fits of excessive passion and appetite, but its proper place was in a hierarchy between the senses and the intellect, anchored in the former and subject to the wisdom and discrimination of the latter. The concept of degree cleared up any questions about the imagination's proper function, and departures from that function, any freedom from reason's supervision, could automatically be assumed troublesome. The ill effects ranged from momentary illusion to insanity. Burton's description of fantasy (the two terms were interchangeable) is such a clear summary of contemporary theory that it is worth quoting in full. Besides the five outward senses, he tells us that there are three inward senses—memory, common sense, and fantasy:

> *Phantasy,* or imagination, which some call *estimative,* or *cogitative,* ... is an inner sense which doth more fully examine the species perceived by *common sense,* of things present or absent, and keeps them longer, recalling them to mind again, or making new of his own. In time of sleep this faculty is free, and many times conceives strange, stupend, absurd shapes, as in sick men we commonly observe. His *organ* is the middle cell of the brain: his objects all the species communicated to him by the *common sense,* by comparison of which he feigns infinite others unto himself. In *melancholy* men this faculty is most powerful and strong, and often hurts,

producing many monstrous and prodigious things, especially if it be stirred up by some terrible object presented to it from *common sense* or *memory*. In Poets and Painters imagination forcibly works, as appears by their several fictions, anticks, images: as Ovid's House of Sleep, Psyche's Palace in Apuleius, &c. In men it is subject and governed by reason, or at least should be; but in brutes it hath no superior and is *ratio brutorum,* all the reason they have.

(*Anatomy of Melancholy,* Pt. I, Sec. 1, Mem. 2, Subsec. 7)[15]

Given such characteristics, the imagination, under any rationalistic system, becomes a sort of moral and epistemological scapegoat. Gianfrancesco Pico della Mirandola, nephew of the famous Pico, in his treatise on the imagination, describes it as the fountain of all vices:

Nor is it hard to prove that universal errors which occur as much in civil life as in the philosophic and Christian life, take their beginnings from the defect of the imagination. The peace of the State is disturbed by ambition, cruelty, wrath, avarice, and lust. But then the depraved imagination is the mother and nurse of ambition. . . . Cruelty, wrath, and passion are born from and nourished by the imagination of an ostensible but deceptive good. . . . What else excites the insatiable thirst for gold? What else kindles the ardor for lust? And what else, if not the deceitful imagination, brings to the fore the other vices which for want of time I omit to mention?[16]

One notices here, as in other Renaissance discussions of imagination, the emphasis placed upon the deceptive character of the faculty. Its pictures are illusory, not true to reality. Behind this lies the Greek sense of fantasy as appearance. For writers

15. Burton, pp. 102–03.
16. Gianfrancesco Pico della Mirandola, *De Imaginatione,* ed. and trans. Harry Caplan (New Haven, 1930), pp. 45–47.

with Platonist leanings, skeptical of all sense data, imagination shares the limitations and deceptions of material reality; it is too close to the senses. With empiricists, however, it fares no better; for them it is too far from the senses, too easily detached. "False shows and suppositions"[17] are what worry Burton, and madmen, as he points out, suffer from a disjunction of senses and imagination:

> As they that drink wine think all runs round, when it is in their own brain, so is it with these men, the fault and cause is inward, as Galen affirms, mad men and such as are near death, have in their eyes images of what they think and see. . . . For the aged have often such hollow and dry brains that they fancy themselves to see that which is not.[18]

Placed midway in a hierarchy and therefore responsible to faculties in opposite directions, imagination was doubly dependent, so that its chief quality, freedom, was precisely what everyone felt should be denied it. This view, embedded in rational philosophy and classical theories of art, was to persist until it was overturned by the Romantics. The following samples of its various expressions are drawn, respectively, from Samuel Parker, Malebranche, and Dr. Johnson:

> I that am too simple or too serious to be cajol'd with the frenzies of a bold and ungovern'd Imagination cannot be perswaded to think the Quaintest plays and sportings of wit to be any real and true knowledge.[19]

17. Burton, *Anatomy of Melancholy*, p. 159.
18. Ibid., p. 257.
19. Samuel Parker, *A Free and Impartial Censure of the Platonick Philosophie* (Oxford, 1666), p. 73. Cited in Donald F. Bond, "Distrust of Imagination in English Neo-Classicism," *Philological Quarterly, 14* (October, 1935), 56.

Les sens et l'imagination sont des sources fécondes et inépui-
sables d'egaraments et d'illusions.[20]

Imagination, a licentious and vagrant faculty, unsusceptible
of limitations, and impatient of restraint, has always en-
deavored to baffle the logician, to perplex the confines of
distinction, and burst the inclosures of regularity.[21]

Each of these censures, however, also contains hints of praise,
the seeds which Romanticism would finally cultivate. The imagination, as Dr. Johnson represents it, sounds Faustian, hero-
ically, if satanically, interesting. Indeed, all the classical, medieval, and Renaissance theories of imagination qualify their
criticism of the faculty in two important ways: they admit its
necessity in the processes of knowledge, and they respect its
power. Both thought and action, Bacon tells us, depend upon
the intermediary power of the imagination:

> The imagination, indeed, on both sides, performs the office of
> agent, or ambassador, and assists alike in the judicial and
> ministerial capacity. Sense commits all sorts of notions to the
> imagination, and the reason after judges of them. In like
> manner reason transmits select and approved notions to the
> imagination before the decree is executed: for imagination
> always precedes and excites voluntary motion.
>
> (*Advancement of Learning,* Bk. V, Chap. 1)[22]

Pico reasons as follows: cognition originates from sense (he
cites Aristotle for this), and all sense impressions are stored in
the fantasy; "therefore we must infer that the behavior of all

20. M. Malebranche, *De la Recherche de la Vérité* (4 vols. Paris,
1772), *2,* Bk. III, 2.
21. Samuel Johnson, *Rambler* 125 (1751) (1824 ed. [London],
p. 217).
22. Bacon, p. 133.

animate beings arises from the nature of the phantasy—the imagination."[23]

Imagination, however, in most views, was more than simply "the storehouse of wit."[24] Pico suggests that it can produce its own forms "out of itself" and that it somehow acts to purify the sense impressions it receives and retains, but he does not pursue the implications of either notion.[25] Sir John Davies thought it part of imagination's function to sort, order, and judge sense impressions. He pictures "a higher region of the braine":

> Where Fantasie, neere hand-maid to the mind,
>   Sits and beholds, and doth discerne them all;
>   Compounds in one, things divers in their kind;
>   Compares the black and white, the great and small.
>
> Besides, those single formes she doth esteeme,
>   And in her ballance doth their values trie;
>   Where some things good, and some things ill doe seem,
>   And neutrall some, in her fantasticke eye.
>
> This busie power is working day and night;
>   For when the outward senses rest doe take.
>   A thousand dreames, fantasticall and light,
>   With fluttring wings doe keepe her still awake.[26]

Elsewhere he calls the fantasy "Wit's looking-glasse," explaining that Wit, in the process of becoming Reason, "Lookes in the

---

23. Pico della Mirandola, *De Imaginatione*, p. 39.

24. Richard Hooker, *Ecclesiastical Polity* (2 vols. London, 1890), 2, 58.

25. Pico della Mirandola, pp. 33, 41.

26. Sir John Davies, "Nosce Teipsum," in *Works*, ed. A. B. Grosart (3 vols. Blackburn, 1869–76), *1*, 111–12. Davies distinguishes between Imagination and Fantasy, equating the former with "Common Sense" as a kind of lower or preliminary Fantasy.

mirror of the Fantasie, / Where all the gatherings of the Senses are."[27]

What begins to be clear is that anyone who wished to undertake a defense of the imagination might easily have done so, drawing upon the inherent contradiction in contemporary theories between the feeling that the imagination was deceitful and destructive, and the creative powers commonly granted it as part of the epistemological hierarchy. A Neoplatonist could have cited Plotinus and Pico to develop the view that the fantasy is that part of man which makes him superior to nature and, like God, a creator of forms and images. Sidney comes very close to such a statement:

> Onely the Poet, disdayning to be tied to any such subjection, lifted up with the vigor of his owne invention, dooth growe in effect another nature, in making things either better then Nature bringeth forth, or, quite a newe, formes such as never were in Nature.[28]

How else is this kind of activity to be carried on, one asks, if not through the creative power of the imagination? But Sidney, despite his intriguing use of the term "invention," does not take this step;[29] the allegiance to reason is too strong and its opposition to the imagination too firmly established. Only two of Shakespeare's contemporaries undertook anything like a defense

27. Ibid., pp. 110, 116.
28. Sidney, "An Apologie for Poetrie," p. 156.
29. The sense in which Sidney uses the word "invention" may be clarified by reference to Gascoigne's "Certayne Notes of Instruction" (1575), where the "first and most necessarie point" in the making of "a delectable poem" is said to be the need "to ground it upon some fine inuention." (Smith, *Elizabethan Critical Essays,* p. 47.) Gascoigne seems to have in mind a basic idea or central conceit around which the poem is built, in which case Invention was not a faculty of the mind but an initial product in the creative process. C. S. Lewis, however, in *The Discarded Image* (London, 1964), thinks that medieval and Renaissance theorists "would have used *invention* where we use *imagination*"

of the imagination. John Marston, in *What You Will,* puts in
the mouth of Quadratus what another character aptly terms a
"Most Phantasticall protection of Phantasticknesse":

> A man can scarce put on a tuckt up cap,
> A button'd frizado sute, skarce eate good meate,
> *Anchoves, caviare,* but hee's *Satyred*
> And term'd Phantasticall by the muddy spawne
> Of slymie Neughtes, when troth, *Phantasticknesse,*
> That which the naturall *Sophysters* tearme
> *Phantusia incomplexa,* is a function
> Even of the bright immortal part of man.
> It is the common passe, the sacred dore,
> Unto the prive chamber of the soule:
> That bar[r]'d: nought passeth past the baser Court
> Of outward scence: by it th'inamorate
> Most lively thinkes he sees the absent beauties
> Of his lov'd mistres.
> By it we shape a new creation,
> Of things as yet unborne, by it wee feede
> Our ravenous memory, our intention feast:
> Slid he thats not Phantasticall's a beast.[30]

The last line reverses the *ratio brutorum* view that beasts have
imagination without reason, drawing legitimately upon the
imagination's place as part of the immortal soul and its acknowl-
edged retentive and creative powers.

(p. 163). He gives no source for this statement and may, in fact, have
the Sidney passage in mind. It is also useful in examining the reason–
imagination opposition to recall that phrases like "right reason" were
sometimes used to broaden the sense of the term and connote the
balanced harmonious mind.

30. John Marston, *Plays,* ed. H. Harvey Wood (3 vols. Edinburgh,
1934–39), 2, 250.

It was George Puttenham, however, who offered the fullest defense of the imagination in his *Arte of English Poesie*. Noting that "phantasticall" had become a contemptuous synonym for poet, he protested, like Marston, against the negative sense of the term:

> For as the evill and vicious disposition of the braine hinders the sounde judgement and discourse of man with busie & disordered phantasies . . . so is that part being well affected, not onely nothing disorderly or confused with any monstrous imaginations or conceits, but very formall, and in his much multiformitie *uniforme,* that is well proportioned, and so passing cleare, that by it as by a glasse or mirrour, are represented unto the soule all maner of bewtifull visions, whereby the inventive parte of the mynde is so much holpen, as without it no man could devise any new or rare thing.[31]

This is clear and straightforward and does not so much confute contemporary views as draw from them the implication that the imagination, when its images are not corrupted or distorted, brings unity out of multiplicity and enables men to create. For Puttenham it is not limited to lovers or madmen or even poets but is characteristic of all human activity:

> And of this sorte of phantasie are all good Poets, notable Captaines strategematique, all cunning artificers, and enginers, all Legislators, Polititiens & Counsellours of estate, in whose exercises the inventive part is most employed and is to the sound & true judgement of man most needful.[32]

Puttenham's defense was available to Shakespeare, but he need not have consulted it to arrive at the same view, since it was a

---

31. George Puttenham, *The Arte of English Poesie,* eds. Gladys Doidge Willcock and Alice Walker (London, 1936), pp. 18–19.

32. Ibid., pp. 19–20.

short step from current epistemological theory and was obscured only by the traditional attitude that imagination somehow interfered with "the sound and true judgement of man."

If we turn to Shakespeare's plays, we find in them frequent reference to the imagination, much of it at first glance along the orthodox lines discussed above. When Hotspur, for instance, is carried away with rebellious anger and excitement, his father, unable to get his attention, remarks:

> Imagination of some great exploit
> Drives him beyond the bounds of patience.
> (*1 Henry IV*, I.3.199–200)

A moment later, his uncle rephrases the same idea:

> He apprehends a world of figures here,
> But not the form of what he should attend.
> (I.3.209–10)

This is standard Elizabethan psychology. Hotspur's imagination has outrun his reason and he is, for the moment, technically insane. His passion is contrasted with the more reasonable behavior of his father and uncle. But the fact remains that, here and elsewhere, it is Hotspur whom we admire, not Worcester or Northumberland. The psychological summary does not tell the whole story because it places no value on the imagination: Hotspur, like Falstaff, outshines the "reasonable" characters in his world.

What is true of Hotspur is true of many Shakespearean characters, most notably the great tragic heroes. If we wish to moralize upon their cases, we can say that each of them errs through excess of imagination. Lear imagines a world very different from the one he lives in; Othello is willing to suppose on the evidence of his own fears and fantasies that his wife has betrayed him; and so on. Coleridge's famous comment on *Hamlet* works out the same idea:

> In Hamlet I conceive him to have wished to exemplify the moral necessity of a due balance between our attention to outward objects, and our meditation on inward thoughts,— a due balance between the real and the imaginary worlds. In Hamlet this balance does not exist.[33]

This, although it brings in the imaginary world, does not quite satisfy, for it suggests that had Hamlet a weaker or more docile imagination things would have been all right, and while there is some truth in that judgment, by itself it simplifies and distorts the play. Moreover, our sympathy and admiration for Hamlet, indeed, his endless fascination for us are all based on that very quality Coleridge picks out—his strong and teeming imagination. Take that away from him and you have only a Laertes or a Fortinbras.

Even Macbeth, butcher and hellhound, has that same vivid imagination which, on the moral level, unseats his reason and makes him an example of overweening ambition and, at the same time, on the psychological level, makes him, among his starts and hallucinations, an interesting and partly sympathetic character. His story is in one sense the case history of a corrupting and deadening imagination, of a man who goes from a sensitivity in which his hair stands up in response to mental images, where "present fears / Are less than horrible imaginings," through a series of evil deeds and accompanying hallucinations, to a point where he has "supp'd full with horrors" and nothing real or imagined can startle his "slaughterous thoughts." His wife's story provides an ironic counterpoint. Brisk and hardheaded, she dismisses his imaginings and attributes his hallucinations to fear rather than conscience. Yet her own sense of guilt,

33. Coleridge, *Coleridge's Shakespearean Criticism*, p. 37.

the imaginative understanding of her acts, is not entirely absent —"Had he not resembled / My father as he slept, I had done't"— and it does not harden and disappear like her husband's, but instead bursts suddenly in upon her. Thus, the contrast between husband and wife is worked out exactly. Macbeth, vividly conscious of his guilt, murders sleep and deprives himself of any respite until he is ruined and defeated. His wife, who has mastered her conscious sense of guilt, is driven to acknowledge it in her sleep. Both are eventually understood in terms of the effects which their acts have upon their respective imaginations.

In Lear's case, the ambiguity of the imagination is even more apparent, for it is expressed in terms of madness. For the Elizabethans, as for us, insanity meant the severing of one's ties to reality. Imagination, no longer serving to link reason and the senses, runs free and wild. This is precisely what happens to Lear. In the farmhouse, where he stages a trial of his daughters with pieces of furniture, he is no longer able to distinguish the elements of his delusion from actual objects. Again, however, we find ourselves pushed beyond the orthodox point of view. As so many commentators on the play have pointed out, it is in his madness that Lear makes the most sense. His freed imagination, having "burst the inclosures of regularity," is the vehicle for the tremendous insights into the human condition which his tragedy affords. The beadle and the whore to whom he speaks in the fields near Dover do not exist, but what he has to say to them deals tellingly with the whole concept of authority and justice in his corrupted kingdom.

It may be objected that only in fiction do madmen speak such wisdom, but it is also true that something in us accepts the convention, acquiesces in the destruction of reason and the exaltation of imagination, even of imagination gone wild. The idea that illusion and reality may be reversed is present in most of us. If there is such a thing as illusion, then there is always the possibility that everything may be illusion, and if there is reality, then anything may be real. We need not be Platonists or skeptics to respond to Hamlet's dilemma or to listen sympathetically to the ravings of Lear. They touch our imaginations and, through them, our entire beings.

It is against this background, as well as in the context of the play, that we must view Theseus' remarks about the imagination. Placed at the beginning of the last act, after the night in the woods and before the performance by the mechanicals, they are the hinge for the final turn taken by the play. They constitute the last direct comment, within the play, on the night in the woods and the introduction both to the play within a play and to the considerations with which we are left when the play itself is over. They are often quoted out of context and too frequently discussed as if they represented the views of the author. I propose to approach them once more, this time with the notion that Shakespeare's views can be determined only, if at all, by differentiating them from what Theseus says.[34]

As Theseus and Hippolyta enter in the last act, we hear her broach the subject of the night in the woods:

> 'Tis strange, my Theseus, that these lovers speak of.
>
> (V.i.i)

There has been some attempt, we gather, to explain what happened, and Hippolyta has been struck by the coincidence of details in the four "dreams." Her bridegroom, however, is ready with an answer:

> More strange than true. I never may believe
> These antique fables nor these fairy toys.
>
> (V.i.2–3)

34. The approach is not original with me. It is suggested by Elizabeth Sewell in *The Orphic Voice,* Pt. 2, sec. 5; by Murray W. Bundy in "Shakespeare and Elizabethan Psychology," *JEGP,* 22 (October 1925), 536; and by Frank Kermode, "The Mature Comedies," p. 219.

While he dismisses the lovers' dreams as having no truth, Theseus at the same time moves the issues into larger ground, for he includes in the realm of untruth the worlds of myth and folklore and art. "Antique" (which is "antick" in Q2 and F1&2) nicely combines the ancient and the irresponsible. Thus, an "antique [old] fable" would be a classical myth, while an "antick [grotesque] fable" would be a tall story or any work of art insufficiently grounded in reality. "Fairy toys" is equally suggestive, this time combining art with folktales and superstitions. Theseus has no need to introduce such topics, except that he seems anxious to set up an opposition between reason and the imagination, as the next lines indicate:

> Lovers and madmen have such seething brains,
> Such shaping fantasies, that apprehend
> More than cool reason ever comprehends.
>
> (V.1.4–6)

The difference between "apprehension" and "comprehension" is clear enough here. To comprehend something is to understand it completely. Since intelligibility is impossible in the absence of reason, Theseus has won his case in advance by loading the terms. Apprehension may be a step toward knowledge, but by itself it is unreliable, the limitation shared by lovers and madmen, and by poets as well, as already implied in the remark about "fables" and "toys" and as made explicit in the next two lines:

> The lunatic, the lover, and the poet
> Are of imagination all compact.
>
> (V.1.7–8)

There follows the famous account of the separate activities of the kindred imaginations. They apprehend, respectively, devils, beauty, and "things unknown." The poet, Theseus admits, puts his experience to some use, but it is still the same kind of false experience he shares with the others.

After we have read or witnessed the four acts that precede these remarks, what are we to think of them? We have seen lunacy and love; we have heard poetry. We know from what has happened within the play that there is some sense in Theseus' remarks; that, as Bottom has put it, "reason and love keep little company together"; that Lysander, swearing to Helena that his reason has moved him to transfer his love to her from Hermia, is ludicrously wrong. We can in part accept the dichotomy and value Theseus' consistent position as a man of reason and common sense.

But one would have to be a fool to leave it at that, for Theseus is also wrong. The lovers' account, both strange and true, is not a dream. We have seen it happen. In the play's terms, there are such things as fairies, and, by extension, there is truth in antique fables and fairy toys, in the shaping fantasies of lovers, poets, and madmen. Moreover, to claim to be on the side of reason, as Lysander's case illustrated, is dangerous. Theseus has conveniently forgotten what we remember hearing in the first act: that he, like the lovers, like Bottom, was once a fairy victim too, led "through the glimmering night" by Titania herself, who has followed his fortunes and come to bless his wedding.

Poor Theseus. His reason is overmatched by the facts of the context in which he attempts to exercise it. A moment later he is mixing up his terminology, allowing imagination to "comprehend":

> Such tricks hath strong imagination
> That, if it would but apprehend some joy,
> It comprehends some bringer of that joy.
>
> (V.1.18–20)

During the interlude, he is willing to employ imagination to amend what he is seeing, giving it a function not unlike comprehension. Finally, as he goes to bed, he says with unconscious irony that it is "almost fairy time." This is metaphorically meant but literally true, and as he leaves the stage the fairies in whom he refuses to believe troop in to bless his house.

All this we see from our superior vantage point within the context of the play. We may add to it what we know when we stand outside the play: that it is a play; that Theseus is a figure from antique fable; that he owes his local habitation, if not his name, to Shakespeare in this instance; that he cannot exist for us except within a fairy toy of some kind; that imagination, not reason, gives him whatever value and interest he has. These reactions grow naturally out of our role as spectators. The reader will recall the earlier image of expanding circles, which applies here as well. Theseus stands within his circle of comprehension and insists, with comic dignity, that that is all there is. By the end of the play, we have learned that that circle is even smaller than we thought.

When Theseus has finished his remarks about the imagination, it is Hippolyta who has the last word. Her speech is thoughtful and pointed. Because Theseus has raised the triple subject, love, madness, and poetry, she seems to speak of all three as well. At least her comment applies very aptly to art:

> But all the story of the night told over,
> And all their minds transfigur'd so together,
> More witnesseth than fancy's images
> And grows to something of great constancy;
> But howsoever, strange and admirable.
>
> (V.1.23–27)

Primarily this says that the lovers' experiences correspond. But it also invokes, through terms like "story" and "constancy," the values of art, the consistent and coherent shape it may give to imaginative experience, differentiating it from the raving of the lunatic and returning it to the realm of actuality.

Shakespeare has again raised the issue of poetry's value. There is no attempt to settle the problem, but in the notion of minds "transfigur'd so together," of images of fancy given "constancy," lies a potential defense of the poet's art. Even well-meaning reasonable men like Theseus do not understand this because they do not know how to value the imagination. But when reason's limitations are shown, as they are here, as indeed they are in *Lear,* then the imagination, and with it poetry, must be readmitted as a way of at least apprehending "More than cool reason ever comprehends." Once again, by comic means, Shakespeare has broken down an orthodox Renaissance dichotomy to force a reexamination of human knowledge and experience. The inquiry touches epistemology, psychology, and ethics, but it also reaches, by a deliberate gesture on the poet's part, into the realm of the aesthetic, so that the questions raised by the play turn back by an imperceptible process to become the play itself. In short, the resolution of the oppugnancy of reason and imagination posed by Theseus is the very context from which he speaks, the poetry into which he is allowed to put it, the play that is his local habitation. It is a happy kind of metamorphosis that allows the poet to meet the strictures against his art by making art of them.

"Formes such as never were"   Lysander, victim of the love-juice, wakens to fall in love with a startled Helena. Here are his first words of explanation:

> Transparent Helena! Nature shows art,
> That through thy bosom makes me see thy heart.
>
> (II.2.104–05)

Lysander's use of the word "art," we may suppose, is an expression of his sense that there is something unusual about his sudden change of affection. But his chief emphasis is on the rightness and propriety of his passion. This is his first glimpse of Helena in the woods, and he can only assume that the natural setting has revealed something that must have been true all along. The moonlight has made Helena "transparent," that is, both brilliantly attractive and exceptionally visible in her essence. In his next speech, Lysander will also invoke reason and maturity, but here it is nature herself who is summoned to justify his mild metamorphosis.

In a sense, of course, Lysander is right. Oberon's flower is remarkable but in no way unnatural. It represents "nature's art," white magic rather than black, not the product of demonic conjuration but simply a special sort of herb available to Oberon's particularly intimate knowledge of nature. Insofar as Oberon and Puck are represented as spirits with magical powers they are also seen, like Prospero's Ariel, as embodiments of natural forces, owing their powers to an art which extends the natural without in any way opposing it.

If Lysander, like the fairies who practice upon him, sees no particular conflict between nature and art, the terms themselves serve to evoke the world of Renaissance literary criticism and the debates that sprang from the repeated attempts to achieve common agreement in the interpretation of critics like Horace and Aristotle. It is a complex world indeed. The terms "nature" and "art" were used in discussions of science and reason, both of which were sometimes labeled "art," as well as in defenses of the instincts and passions (e.g. Montaigne's "naturall inclinations"). Even if we limit ourselves to the areas of aesthetic dispute, we must remember that "art" might be used to mean craft, ornament, impropriety, exaggeration, or the ability to express the Ideal, while "nature," on the other side, could stand for inspiration, simplicity, propriety, verisimilitude, or the relatively meaningless particular. And even when the terms are correctly paired and rightly understood, we stand in danger of losing ourselves in exceptional thickets of ambiguity. The Elizabethans, for instance, were almost always inclined to favor nature over art in theory at the same time that they elaborated a remarkable artificial tradition in practice. The pastoral mode is perhaps the best example of this kind of apparent contradiction. It contains such artificial praise of the natural and affects such an unconvincing dislike of the artificial that its case for naturalness and simplicity tends to evaporate, leaving only its charm and our almost reluctant enjoyment behind.

Shakespeare shows familiarity with the art–nature conflict as well as with the various means used to decide or resolve it. One of these is simply to declare in favor of art. "Heaven-bred poesy," as depicted by Proteus, enjoys a clear superiority:

> For Orpheus' lute was strung with poets' sinews,
> Whose golden touch could soften steel and stones;
> Make tigers tame, and huge leviathans
> Forsake unsounded deeps to dance on sands.
> *(Two Gentlemen,* III.2.78–81)

Here, art in its ideal expression has the power to alter the natural for its own purposes. The poet and painter in *Timon,* who seem to be figures of fun, touch on the same notion more modestly but no less assuredly:

> It tutors nature: artificial strife
> Lives in these touches, livelier than life.
> (I.1.37–38)

Against this we must balance the Shakespearean suggestions that art and the artificial must be subjected to the natural. The whole of *As You Like It* is instructive in this regard, as are Hamlet's appeals to "the modesty of nature" and the Chorus' reminder to the audience in *Henry V* that they are "Minding true things by what their mock'ries be."

Most relevant to this study, however, are Shakespearean at-

tempts to break down the art–nature dichotomy or dissolve it
altogether. We have already examined, in connection with the
topic of dreams, Cleopatra's conversation with Dolabella in the
last act of *Antony and Cleopatra*. Here are her words again:

> Nature wants stuff
> To vie strange forms with fancy; yet, t'imagine
> An Antony were nature's piece 'gainst fancy,
> Condemning shadows quite.
>
> (V.2.97–100)

Nature is here represented as ordinarily inferior to fancy in its
inventiveness but superior in its fabrication of Antony. Its
triumph, moreover, makes of it an artist; it "imagines" Antony.
Nature seems to win its rivalry with art by adopting the op-
ponent's methods. The converse of this idea is touched on by
Hamlet: the closer "The Mouse-trap" can come to the deed of
the guilty creature watching it, the more potency and truth it
contains as art. Art and nature, imitating one another, tend to
merge.

A more direct attempt to resolve the opposition can be found
in the famous conversation about flowers in *The Winter's Tale*.
In a scene shot through with references to disguise and metamorphosis, Perdita objects to the artificial breeding of flowers
and Polixenes answers in its defense:

> Yet nature is made better by no mean
> But nature makes that mean. So, over that art
> Which you say adds to nature, is an art
> That nature makes . . .
>
> This is an art
> Which does mend nature—change it rather; but
> The art itself is nature.
>
> (IV.4.89–97)

This is essentially Cicero's compromise,[35] and it was familiar enough in the Renaissance not only in Italy through men like Speroni,[36] but in Shakespeare's England, as Madelaine Doran has pointed out,[37] through the good offices of George Puttenham. The final chapter of *The Arte of English Poesie* is a remarkably sensitive discussion of the whole question of artifice. Puttenham suggests a multiple and variable relationship between nature and art. Sometimes art is "an ayde and coadiutor" (as in gardening and medicine), sometimes an alterer and surmounter, sometimes "onely a bare immitatour," sometimes even "an encountrer and contrary to nature." This whole range is available to the poet; "it is not altogether with him as with the crafts man, nor altogether otherwise than with the crafts man":

> But for that in our maker or Poet, which restes only in devise and issues from an excellent sharpe and quick invention, holpen by a cleare and bright phantasie and imagination, he is . . . even as nature her selfe working by her owne peculiar vertue and proper instinct and not by example or meditation or exercise as all other artificers do, is then most admired when he is most naturall and least artificiall.[38]

Ben Jonson echoes these views in *Timber* when he says of poets and painters that

> they both invent, feign, and devise many things, and accommodate all they invent to the use and service of Nature. . . .

---

35. See the discussion in Arthur O. Lovejoy and others, *A Documentary History of Primitivism and Related Ideas* (Baltimore, 1935), *1*, chap. 9, and Hiram Haydn, *The Counter-Renaissance* (2 vols. New York, 1950), pp. 469–70.

36. See Baxter Hathaway's discussion of the problem in *The Age of Criticism: The Late Renaissance in Italy* (Ithaca, 1962), pp. 437 ff.

37. Doran, *Endeavors of Art*, pp. 59–60.

38. Puttenham, *Arte of English Poesie*, pp. 303–07.

They both are born artificers, not made. Nature is more powerful in them than study.[39]

Between the writing of these two passages, Elizabethan poets and dramatists had more or less achieved the ideal being expressed. They learned to subdue rhetoric in such a way that it did not call attention to itself, to employ artifice so that it seemed to complement rather than contend with the naural. As Hardin Craig says, "There is no longer any creaking of the machine."[40] Shakespeare himself played the greatest role in this closing of the art–nature split. There seems no reason to doubt that he was conscious of this synthesis as a part of his artistic achievement. Again and again he dares to call attention to the issue as a means of dismissing it. Fabian, laughing at the trick played upon Malvolio, remarks:

> If this were play'd upon a stage now, I could condemn it as an improbable fiction.
>
> > (*Twelfth Night*, III.4.140)

The mention of the discrepancy between art and reality forestalls our criticism and strengthens our sense of their bond. And the artist's awareness of the problem makes us feel that he can be trusted to solve it.

The same sort of moment occurs at the end of *Love's Labour's Lost*, when Biron says:

> Our wooing doth not end like an old play;
> Jack hath not Gill. These ladies' courtesy
> Might well have made our sport a comedy.
>
> > (V.2.883–85)

This speech rescues the play from a genuine difficulty. On the one hand, we have sat through a very artificial sort of comedy

39. Jonson, *Works, 8,* 609–10.
40. Hardin Craig, *The Enchanted Glass* (New York, 1936), p. 166.

and are relieved to see it end with the intrusion of reality. On the other hand, we are uneasy at the idea that nature is forcing itself upon art. Biron's observation is nearly our own and reminds us that we are still in the presence of artifice, an artifice which has the strength to call attention to itself, and that this same artifice has been brought remarkably close to the real, the natural. The gap disappears, and one comic marriage—the marriage of art and reality—takes place at the expense of some others. When the king reminds Biron that they have only a year to wait for their proper resolution, he answers, "That's too long for a play." This can be accompanied by a wink at the audience. The characters step out of their roles; the play remains.

How, we may now ask, is the art–nature dichotomy employed and resolved in *A Midsummer Night's Dream?* An appropriate place to begin is with our sense of nature in the play, a sense which, as was indicated earlier, is greater, richer, and more fully particularized than in any previous play. Nature's abundant presence in the scenes in the woods is clearly central both to the atmosphere in which the events of the play take place and to the playwright's expression of man's relationship with the natural world. In effect, the *Dream* takes up the topics of pastoralism while avoiding the compromising artificiality of the convention. The woods, it is true, are very artfully presented and filled with the mysterious and the bizarre by virtue of the presence of the fairies. But Shakespeare has carefully set up a strong crosscurrent of homely and realistic detail which serves to convince his audience that the woods are not merely literary, at least not literary in any conventional sense. This is the reason, of course, for the heavy doses of folklore in the play and for the companionship of Puck and Oberon. Nature and art can coexist here without any apparent discord, so that we forget to think of them separately. Oberon is mysterious, but his chief device for magic is the very familiar pansy. Titania is exotic, but her pensioners are merely cowslips. Puck harries the homespuns but admits himself that it is their own fear that makes senseless things appear to be hostile to them (III.2.28). Art shows nature so skillfully that it does in fact begin to seem, to return to Lysander's phrase, that nature shows art, that we are being shown not an "improbable fiction" but something which has always existed just beyond our notice. Our sense of the meaning and value of nature is both expanded and intensified.

It is tempting, in light of this, to connect Shakespeare's view of nature with those of Renaissance thinkers who saw it as boundless, mysterious, and beyond the reach and laws of reason. Pico and Bruno, for example, held such views, views which mark them as "romanticists of the Counter-Renaissance."[41] For them, infinite nature was sacred, an aspect of the infinite God. One wonders whether such a view would produce a comedy like the *Dream*. More persuasive as a parallel is the naturalism of a man like Montaigne:

> Such a naturalist as Montaigne shares this view of Nature as infinite, and believes that we know nothing of God's intent or functioning principles. But his Nature is not pantheistic; it is rather "neutralized." She is the indifferent mother of an infinite diversity and mutability, and her works are all equally good, all the children of her fertility in a world innocent of comprehensive systematizing and universal regulative principles of degree, vocation, etc. She is, if you will, Venus Geniatrix [sic], mother of instincts and senses, of biological motivation and uninhibited fertility. In addition to Montaigne, Lorenzo Valla and Rabelais had sung her praises; she is also celebrated in the primitivistic poetry of Ronsard and the young John Donne.[42]

41. Haydn, *The Counter-Renaissance,* p. 464.
42. Ibid., p. 465.

If Shakespeare and Montaigne share this view of nature, they
are not always led to draw the same implications from it.
Shakespeare cannot, like Montaigne, be called a primitivist,
nor is his distrust of reason so extensive. He does not so much
pull reason from its pedestal as move it over to make room for
imagination and, by implication, art. The play makes us feel
that sooner or later reason loses itself in nature just as the lovers
are lost in the forest. While nature is not to be circumscribed
by man, she is none the less essentially benevolent; natural instincts are to be trusted. Art's role must be to make the best
possible use of the natural, as Theseus the hunter creates
harmony in the western valley by matching the voices of his
hounds. Man is always a better artist than he knows. And poetry,
with its companions, mythology and folklore, perhaps may
penetrate further into nature's mysteries than philosophy by
nature of its affinity. As Montaigne himself says:

> Have I not seen this divine saying in Plato, that Nature is
> nothing but an aenigmaticall poesie? As a man might say, an
> overshadowed and darke picture, entershining with an in-
> finit varietie of false lights, to exercise our conjectures.[43]

Poetry, less presumptuous than philosophy, mirrors this picture
and comes closer to the truth.

I think this view of the nature–art relationship can be
ascribed to Shakespeare with considerable assurance and can
be found in *Lear* and *The Winter's Tale* as well, thus giving
Shakespeare's thought more consistency and continuity than is
sometimes granted by his commentators. If that claim seems
excessive, we can at least observe the way in which the view of
nature as "aenigmaticall poesie" has found its way into *A Midsummer Night's Dream*.

Almost every element points toward it. The lovers, silly and

43. M. de Montaigne, "An Apologie of Raymond Sebond," *Florio's
Montaigne*, Tudor Translations (3 vols. London, 1892–93), 2, 249.

artificial before they leave the city, find themselves confronted in the woods with forces they do not begin to understand, forces which are at once within and outside them. Eventually, order is restored and they are purged of most of their strained and conventional characteristics and allowed a more natural harmony, but their limitations remain because they do not recognize the role that nature plays in their behavior. The foolish artisans, as aspiring illusionists, fare very badly for the same kind of reason. They do not understand how the natural and the artificial can be made to interact. Their attempts at verisimilitude are clearly unrealistic, and their artistic flights are disastrously divorced from their audience's sense of what is natural. Pyramus and Thisby's night in the woods is stiff with artifice and convention, approaching reality only at those moments when it fails as illusion. It helps here to remember that one sense of "natural" in Shakespeare is "foolish." As artists, the clowns are hopelessly natural; as naturals, delightfully mechanical. On a much higher level is Theseus, whose activities and pronouncements come to stand for a limited artifice in the midst of an unlimited nature, a respectable view that is far less comprehensive than the play that contains it, a contrast which makes the play both artful and natural in ways that Theseus would fail to understand.

Finally, there are those moments when the playwright, by way of expressing his confidence and winning our approbation, calls attention to his play as artifice. If we remember the passage from *Love's Labour's Lost* quoted just above, we will have a better understanding of Puck's words as he arranges the correct tableaux for the coming of dawn:

> Jack shall have Jill;
> Naught shall go ill;
> The man shall have his mare again, and all shall be well.
> (III.2.461–63)

This wooing *will* end like an old play. We are encouraged to make that observation even as we watch the arrangements being made. Throughout, Puck has been a kind of stage manager for us, with a vocabulary—"actor," "auditor," "sport," "fond pageant" —to match. As the one who has heightened our sense of the play as play, it is fitting that he should make the final gesture in the epilogue, speaking both as actor and character and inviting our participation in the dream and our applause as spectators. Art, when it does not pose as something else, is not afraid to call itself art because "the art itself is nature." Several oppositions are dealt with at once in such moments: that between art and nature as well as subsidiary distinctions such as feigning in poetry and truth in other forms of knowledge, and the illusion of the stage and the reality of the world. Such debates do not trouble this play. They are mentioned or touched upon as a means of strengthening and enriching what is in effect a self-vindicating art. This is Sidney's poet, who "dooth growe in effect another nature, in making things either better than Nature bringeth forth, or, quite a newe, formes such as never were in Nature." He is not nature's secretary or apprentice, but rather her partner, "hee goeth hand in hand with Nature."[44]

Oppositions   To the preceding group of intellectual oppositions we will add one or two which will require less discussion. The first of these is the traditional comic conflict between love and law, or, to take our terms from the play, between doting, irrational love-in-idleness and sane and sanctioned love within the Athenian framework. If I have granted less space to love than to other themes, it is because the thematic uses are more familiar and perhaps less central to this play than to other Shakespearean comedies. The quartet of young Athenians presents us with the well-known contrasts between sight and blindness, infatuation and settled love, youthful license and parental

44. Sidney, "An Apologie for Poetrie," p. 156.

authority. The Pyramus and Thisby story reminds us, glancingly, that such confusions can have disastrous consequences. The falling-out of Oberon and Titania alters the elements and seasons. And in the affair between Bottom and Titania we have what is surely the funniest example of infatuation ever brought to the stage. The effect of the whole is to make us feel that there is no wholly reliable answer to the dilemmas of love. Bottom, waking last and jumbling a passage from St. Paul, is, in the words of Frank Kermode,

> there to tell us that the blindness of love, the dominance of the mind over the eye, can be interpreted as a means to grace as well as to irrational animalism; that the two aspects are, perhaps, inseparable.[45]

Here, as elsewhere, familiar ideas are undermined in favor of a more complex and less settled approach to experience. The safe and sane married love of Theseus and Hippolyta may be the wisest answer; certainly it makes the most appropriate comic ending. But we are not to forget or ignore the alternatives. The amoral, hedonistic side of love is not defeated, and Campion's sentiments persist:

> All you that love, or loved before,
>   The fairy queen Proserpina
> Bids you increase that loving humor more;
>   They that yet have not fed
>   On delight amorous,
>   She vows that they shall lead
>   Apes in Avernus.[46]

45. Kermode, "The Mature Comedies," p. 219. See also Chap. 4, "Orpheus in Praise of Blind Love," in Edgar Wind, *Pagan Mysteries in the Renaissance* (London, 1948).

46. Thomas Campion, *Works,* ed. Percival Vivian (Oxford, 1909), p. 17.

Finally, through the opposed settings of the play we get a series of oppositions which takes us still further into the philosophical divisions of the time. The Athens of Theseus seems to stand for order and containment, and these values, we know, had great appeal. Sir Thomas Elyot speaks for his age:

In every thyng is ordre, and without ordre may be nothing stable or permanent.[47]

The difficulty, if there is one, is that the universe of this comedy is not one in which "In every thyng is ordre." Oberon's woods, in love as in everything else, are characterized by anarchy and license. The opposition remains unresolved because Shakespeare does not here, as he does, for example, in the last act of *The Merchant of Venice,* remind us of a universal harmony surviving and encompassing any earthly disorder. Nor may we take such a universe for granted. As Hiram Haydn has shown, the debate between freedom and limitation, to use his terms, was very much alive and very much an issue—an issue divisive enough so that its resolution could not be assumed.[48] Those Shakespeare plays that specifically treat of nature—more precisely, the nature of nature—plays such as *Lear, As You Like It,* and *The Tempest,* all posit a universe which has neither order nor discernible limits, pitting that notion against the older world-view inherited from the Middle Ages. Since *Dream* is the first of Shakespeare's plays to treat the issue and to suggest the radical position, we are surely justified in taking it more seriously than it has been taken in the past.

It seems appropriate, at this point, to list the various sets of oppositions which are to be found in *A Midsummer Night's*

47. Sir Thomas Elyot, *The Boke Named the Governour,* ed. Foster Watson (London, 1907), p. 4.
48. See chapters 6 and 7 of Haydn, *The Counter-Renaissance,* passim.

Dream. We should begin with the symbolic pairs of contrasts expressed in the settings and the leading images:

Dark	Light
Night	Day
Moon	Sun
Woods	City
Fairy	Mortal
Fluid	Solid
Ether	Matter

The last two pairs, somewhat more abstract, are concretely expressed in the water imagery and in the contrasts between the airy lightness of the fairy characters and the "mortal grossness" of men like Bottom. Even the names (e.g. "Snout" vs. "Cobweb") contribute to our sense of the differences.

From these concrete pairs of opposites, as well as from direct reference, rise the abstract pairs discussed in this chapter:

Dream	Waking
Shadow	Substance
Illusion	Reality
Imagination	Reason
Madness	Sanity
Art	Nature
Feigning	Truth
Stage	World
Love	Law
Freedom	Limitation
Anarchy	Order

It is quite an impressive list for any play, much less a "gossamer" comedy filled with "native woodnotes wild." Even as we examine the various terms in their pairings, they begin to break down and mingle under the playwright's influence, some more readily than others. It is time now to examine more closely the means by which Shakespeare mediates between these sets of apparent opposites.

"I wot not by what power / But by some power it is"   Very little has been said thus far about one of the main elements of *A Midsummer Night's Dream,* its emphasis on change and transformation. Elizabeth Sewell has described the theme:

> Forms in transformation—forms in nature and in the mind—are part of the *Midsummer Night's Dream.* . . . The two meet in Bottom's interlude with Titania: forms as operative powers in natural phenomena, and forms as instruments of the thinking mind. Behind these, however, the whole of nature is seen to be in movement. Everything is changing.[49]

A glance at the exposition of the play will reveal how thoroughly its atmosphere is permeated with figures of change and metamorphosis. The opening lines inform us that Theseus and Hippolyta are awaiting a monthly transformation, the new moon, and the moon itself is hung before us as a familiar emblem of alteration. Hippolyta's response to her lover's impatience suggests a merging of day and night, light and darkness, and Theseus, taking her up, calls for the alteration of melancholy to merriment and war to love. Egeus enters with his complaint that Lysander has bewitched and transformed Hermia, "stol'n the impression of her fantasy" and "Turn'd her obedience . . . to stubborn harshness." Theseus reminds her that this power is reserved to her father, "To whom you are but as a form in wax," and she, in her spirited disputation of this, wonders at her own behavior: "I know not by what power I am made bold." Theseus, explaining her choices of punishment, draws a contrast between the static existence of the nun, removed from nature and hymning the suddenly "cold" and "fruitless" moon, and that of the rose "distill'd," existing in a world of change and procreation.

49. Sewell, *The Orphic Voice,* pp. 139–40.

A few lines later, we learn that Demetrius has made Helena "dote" upon him, that he too can be characterized as change-able, "this spotted and inconstant man." The lovers, left alone, begin their duet on "the course of true love," and its fragility in this unstable world is linked to shadows, dreams, and "the lightning in the collied night." When Helena enters, we learn that she wishes to be literally "translated" into Hermia so as to regain Demetrius' affection, and her soliloquy takes fickleness as its subject:

> Things base and vile, holding no quantity,
> Love can transpose to form and dignity
>
> .   .   .
>
> And therefore is Love said to be a child,
> Because in choice he is so oft beguil'd.
> As waggish boys in game themselves forswear,
> So the boy Love is perjur'd everywhere;
> For ere Demetrius look'd on Hermia's eyne,
> He hail'd down oaths that he was only mine;
> And when this hail some heat from Hermia felt,
> So he dissolv'd, and show'rs of oaths did melt.
> (I.1.232–45)

Here, as elsewhere, inconstancy and change are seen as analogues not only of unthinking and childish behavior, but of natural processes—hail, sunshine, the various states water assumes—as well. The effect is to suggest that what is true of fickle lovers and children is in fact characteristic of the whole world as we know it—reality, if you will. Later on, in the woods, as Oberon and Titania speak of the transformations of weather and land-scape effected by their behavior, we find nothing extraordinary in their embodiment of the power of mutation. As extensions or essences of nature it is right that the fairies should alter their shapes, wander everywhere, quarrel over changelings, and alternately hinder and help the mortals. Puck in his many transformations is more natural than Bottom, who is the victim of a discrepancy between his metamorphic ambitions—to be a tyrant, a lover, a heroine, a lion, a nightingale—and his actual limitations. His only change will take place with Puck's assistance, and it will be, at that, merely an expression of his basic nature, a kind of purification that allows him, with the aid of Titania's change, to fumble through the lover's part until daybreak.

There are, in fact, two kinds of change in the play, two means suggested by which a person or a thing may be transfigured. The first is the alteration of characteristics, physical and otherwise, at the bidding of some powerful force: Puck becomes a stool; the pansy becomes a sacred and powerful herb; Bottom is changed to an ass. The second involves a character, object, or concept, through association or actual merging, with some opposite or unlike character or quality: love is turned to hate; nature becomes art; tragedy turns to comedy; Bottom is made the paramour of the fairy queen. The first sort of change, actual metamorphosis, seems at first glance more remarkable, but since it usually involves physical rather than essential transformation, it is actually less so. Bottom changed to an ass is but a short step, a revelation of inner qualities already familiar to us, while Bottom as the consort of Titania is a huge leap, so great that we feel he never truly makes it: just as the "marriage" is probably never consummated, so is the transformation incomplete.

Both metamorphosis, sudden individual change, and "marriage," the merging of apparent opposites, express the mutable and uncontainable nature of the play, although the second may have more lasting effects than the first. Lysander, who began by standing for "true love," undergoes two changes of affection during the night, but marriage to Hermia, the play suggests (although it does not insist), will offer a more permanent change and a greater stability. The ending catches all the characters, in proper comic fashion, in a swing toward constancy, but this is not the same as saying that their world has suddenly grown stable and reliable. In Athens there is order, but Athens is less permanent and less natural than the wild, changeable woods. The natural magic by which sudden alterations and gradual changes always exist as possibilities is itself the one great constant in the play.

In such a world, it is not difficult to see how Shakespeare has managed to question and even to resolve the opposites examined in this chapter. How are we to say with assurance what madness is when a sudden change in reality can make it sanity? How can we distinguish shadow from substance if they marry, interchange, and partake of each other? Knowledge, apparently, must drift with nature, adjusting itself to sudden transformations, and the poet, who steers through shifting appearances by analogies and correspondences, is a truer pilot than the philosopher with his heavy categorical anchors. Again it seems pertinent to invoke Montaigne as an eloquent parallel:

> The world runnes all on wheeles. All things therein moove without intermission; yea the earth, the rockes of Caucasus, and the Pyramides of Egypt, both with the publike and their own motion. Constancy itself is nothing but a languishing and wavering dance. I cannot settle my object; it goeth so unquietly and staggering, with a natural drunkennesse.[50]

The figure of the staggering drunkard used here belongs in the same category with the lunatic, lover, and poet so prematurely dismissed by Theseus. The room that whirls about him is a truer picture of the dance of matter than the sober man can know. The images which support Montaigne's arguments in such pas-

50. Opening paragraph, Montaigne, "Of Repenting," *Florio, 3*, p. 21.

sages come from the same clusters which inform the poetry of the *Dream:*

> In few, there is no constant existence, neither of our being, nor of the objects. And we, and our judgment, and all mortall things else do uncessantly rowle, turne, and passe away. Thus can nothing be certainely established, nor of the one, nor of the other, both the judgeing and the judged being in continuall alteration and motion. We have no communication with being; for every human nature is ever in the middle betweene being borne and dying; giving nothing of it selfe but an obscure apparence and shadow, and an uncertain and weake opinion. And if perhaps you fix your thought to take its being; it would be even, as if one should go about to graspe the water: for, how much the more he shal close and presse that, which by its own nature is ever gliding, so much the more he shal loose what he would hold and fasten.[51]

Such a view calls reason into doubt and serves, by implication, to exalt the imagination, itself a metamorphic agent capable of grasping and expressing change:

> Thus, seeing all things are subject to passe from one change to another; reason, which therein seeketh a real subsistence, findes her selfe deceived as unable to apprehend any thing subsistent or permanent; forsomuch as each thing either commeth to a being, and is not yet altogether; or beginneth to dy before it be borne.[52]

Spotted and inconstant, elusive as water, nature slides by us as we watch or read the play, and the familiar categories by which we

---

51. Montaigne, "Apologie," 2, 329. For Montaigne, these strictures against reason led on to fideism. Whether they had the same effect on Shakespeare is an interesting question, but not a part of my contention here.

52. Ibid.

judge experience waver, alter, merge, and separate again before our eyes in a "languishing and wavering dance." It is a vision of inconstancy, but a coherent one, something, as Hippolyta reminds us, of great constancy.

The coherence and constancy are in the poet's art, and they spring from his consistent use of the metamorphic principle as a device not only for reflecting experience but for controlling it and expressing its unity. A metaphor, like a simile, discloses a relationship; unlike a simile, however, it presses forward to an identification, and, for a moment, an imaginative transformation takes place, a metamorphosis. One thing has become another, and the change has heuristic benefits; from it we derive meaning, pleasure, a sense of unity in the midst of diversity. The poet, at such moments, is seen as a conjurer or magician able to summon or alter forms at will, a master of a protean existence.

We are more accustomed to speak of this process in connection with poetry and the arts of language than with drama, but surely it is the very stuff of theatrical expression as well, of movement, dance, pantomime, the simplest mimicry. When we see a play, a wooden stage is transformed into something else—a woods, a palace, an island—and people whom we know are actors exchange their ordinary identities for others. Within the action of the drama are many more changes. A man who pretends to be a friend is an enemy; a fat knight pretends to be a robber, a king, a prince, a warrior; a sane man feigns madness. These metaphors move us from the particular to the universal by seeming to signify truths, basic correspondences which the world is always reenacting.

If we think of drama in this way, as enacted metaphor, we can see that its poetry usually represents the culmination, the distilled expression in language of the meaningful identifications we have watched on the stage. Here are some familiar examples of such dramatic metaphors:

The art itself is nature.

I dreamt there was an Emperor Antony.

All the world's a stage.

Upon such sacrifices, my Cordelia,
The gods themselves throw incense.

I see their knavery. This is to make an ass of me.

The last of these is from our play. A closer examination of its context will reveal the process by which dramatic metaphors take shape.

Bottom is an ass. This metaphor is latent in his characterization from the start, and its dramatic value is achieved when it comes true, when it is acted out before us. The moment is accompanied by language that exploits the humor and explores the adequacy of the identification. Bottom's asininity lies in his perfect ignorance of his limitations and the concomitant absurdity of his pride and self-confidence. These qualities, at the moment of revelation, are maintained, even intensified:

Bot. Why do they run away? This is a knavery of them to make me afeard.
Enter Snout
Snout. O Bottom, thou art chang'd! What do I see on thee?
Bot. What do you see? You see an ass-head of your own, do you? (*Exit Snout*)
Enter Quince
Quin. Bless thee, Bottom! bless thee! Thou art translated.
(*Exit*)
Bot. I see their knavery. This is to make an ass of me; to fright me, if they could. But I will not stir from this place, do what they can.

(III.1.115 f.)

The identification is achieved and maintained, and Bottom, the complete ass, is ready to move on into the next metaphor, the one the play has reiterated several times and will now enact most thoroughly: love is blind.

It might be noted that the correspondence between the successful play that is the *Dream* and the failure that is "Pyramus and Thisby" is maintained in this area too. The mechanicals are far too ambitious in their dramatic metaphors: men changed into walls and moons, a Thisby with a "monstrous little voice," a lion that roars like (here simile enters) a sucking dove or a nightingale. From these confusions they produce identifications which are not to be believed:

> Sweet moon, I thank thee for thy sunny beams.
>
> (V.1.277)

These linguistic failures illustrate the dramatic failures, "hot ice and wondrous strange snow," inadequate metamorphoses which do not release meaning or energy and which even serve to destroy the primary metaphor of theatrical illusion.

The concept of metaphor as the very basis of drama and poetry, as "one of the vital and basic powers of human thinking, a power which works by means of a constant play in which the mind singles out and matches figures, perceived, invented, and inherited,"[53] is modern in its articulation. Renaissance theorists could conceive of figurative language only as decoration, never as substance. Even Puttenham, who stumbled into the correct defense of imagination by relating it to all useful activity, could not take the further step of exploring the value of the tropological modes of thought. Of "Ornament Poeticall" he wrote:

53. Elizabeth Sewell, *The Human Metaphor* (Notre Dame, Ind., 1964), p. 11.

> This ornament we speake of is given to it by figures and
> figurative speeches, which be the flowers as it were and
> coulours that a Poet setteth upon his language by arte, as
> the embroderer doth his tone and perle.[54]

And there, for all intents and purposes, the matter rested. Occasionally, paging through the piles of literary disputation that
came out of Italy, one catches hints of what poets have always
intuitively known about their method, but they are only hints.
Bulgarini, for example, saw that metaphor expressed an actual
relationship and was in that sense "true," which led him to con-
clude that it had more to do with the intellect than with the
suspect imagination:

> The true form which is the essence of a metaphor is not some
> power of our mind, but rather the similitude and the con-
> formity which is found between diverse things, and the
> intellect, not the fantasy, is what produces the metaphor,
> and words are the materials with which it is produced.[55]

But this is as far as he goes with the notion. He is merely setting
up a criterion against which he can criticize Dante for calling
his poem a dream! For want of proper soil, the seed fails to take
root.

The concepts of metamorphosis and mutability were not
taken much further. A strain of mysticism did exist in the
Renaissance which exalted the changing and variable qualities
of man and nature. It was Pico who wrote, "He who cannot
attract Pan, approaches Proteus in vain," and of whom Edgar
Wind says:

> In Pico's oration On the Dignity of Man, man's glory is de-
> rived from his mutability. The fact that his orbit of action

54. Puttenham, *Arte of English Poesie,* p. 138.
55. Quoted in Hathaway, *The Age of Criticism,* p. 358.

is not fixed like that of angels or of animals, gives him the
power to transform himself into whatever he chooses and
become a mirror of the universe. He can vegetate like a plant,
rage like a brute, dance like a star, reason like an angel, and
surpass them all by withdrawing into the hidden centre of his
own spirit where he may encounter the solitary darkness of
God. "Who would not admire this chameleon?" . . . Mutability, in Pico's view, is the secret gate through which the universal invades the particular. Proteus persistently transforms
himself because Pan is inherent in him.[56]

This did not lead Pico, however, to a theory of poetry, nor do
we find the other Neoplatonists developing the idea. Pico's
disciple and nephew, Gianfrancesco, was "violently antipoetic
in the best Neo-Platonic tradition."[57]

It would have been difficult, in fact, was difficult for the
admirers of Ovid to say just what they saw in him to respect
and emulate. In fact, it has always been hard to answer the
charge that Ovid is merely a superficial retailer of myth in the
Metamorphoses, because anyone who makes it will not easily
be persuaded that the concept of metamorphosis, Proteus in
Pan, is central to an understanding of man and nature and their
relationship, as well as an accurate paradigm of human thought.
Ovid's most distinguished admirers have been fellow poets—
Chaucer, Shakespeare, Goethe, and Rilke; they have not had to
formulate theories to explain their attraction, since, as poets,
its basis was immediately and instinctively clear to them. The
following exchange in *As You Like It* is crucial to any understanding of Shakespeare's attitude:

56. Wind, *Pagan Mysteries,* pp. 158, 161. The entire chapter, "Pan
and Proteus," is relevant.
57. Bernard Weinberg, *A History of Literary Criticism in the Italian
Renaissance* (2 vols. Chicago, 1961), *1,* 255.

Touch. I am here with thee and thy goats, as the most capricious poet, honest Ovid, was among the Goths.

Jaques (aside). O knowledge ill-inhabited, worse than Jove in a thatch'd house!

Touch. When a man's verses cannot be understood, nor a man's good wit seconded with the forward child understanding, it strikes a man more dead than a great reckoning in a little room. Truly, I would the gods had made thee poetical.

Aud. I do not know what poetical is. Is it honest in deed and word? Is it a true thing?

Touch. No, truly; for the truest poetry is the most feigning, and lovers are given to poetry; and what they swear in poetry may be said, as lovers, they do feign.

(III.3.7–22)

Here is another dramatic metaphor, with Touchstone as the poet, Audrey as his audience, Jaques as a hidden and better audience, and "honest" Ovid, among the goats and Goths, a metaphor within a metaphor, as a kind of archetype for the figure of the poet. The truth of the passage is self-demonstrative: Shakespeare's audience could not possibly have unraveled the puns, caught the reference to Marlowe, and understood the sense in which the truest poetry is the most feigning, as they watched the play. But the playwright's acceptance of the situation is good-humored, based on a thorough understanding of his art and the limitations of his audience. "Be it as it may be," says Touchstone, "I will marry thee." Those who still insist on Shakespeare's natural genius and his unselfconscious art, as if he were a kind of inspired booby, should be made to reread and explicate such passages until they recant. The mind that was capable of drawing together the diverse ideas and experiences of its age into dazzling organic wholes was also capable, here

and elsewhere, of glancing briefly but directly at its methods of
operation:

> Shakespeare picks up precisely what Bacon wants to reject—
> poetry, theater, dreams, and shadows—with an immense re-
> spect for each, and presents through them a vision of *his*
> method, a mythological vision of the relationship between
> man's mind and the natural universe.[58]

58. Sewell, *The Orphic Voice,* p. 114.

Epilogue

UCH MORE, NO DOUBT, REMAINS TO be said about *A Midsummer Night's Dream* than has been said in this study. But my own claims and conclusions about the play have been registered in the preceding chapters. What seems appropriate, by way of epilogue, is an attempt to draw back from the play and view it from a greater distance in the light of what has been said about it here. I shall content myself with some suggestions about the particular interest the play may now be seen to hold for the intellectual historian and the student of Shakespeare's art.

Against the large backdrop of its time, *A Midsummer Night's Dream* can be said to reflect with remarkable accuracy the historical and cultural transitions of the age. It partakes of the values of the Renaissance, but it also looks forward to the newer age which historians of English literature call Jacobean and art historians call Mannerist and Baroque. If we find ourselves examining the latter terms, it is because the art historians have done the most to demonstrate how crucial to the arts was the sixteenth century's revised concept of the universe and of man's place in it. Otto Benesch writes:

> Copernicus achieved the theoretical formulation of a notion of space which developed at about the same time in painting from Altdorfer to Bruegel—a notion of space which suggests the grandeur of the universe by man's eccentric position in it.[1]

1. Otto Benesch, *The Art of the Renaissance in Northern Europe* (Cambridge, Mass., 1945), p. 126.

Human figures had occupied the central foreground in paintings and prints; artists began to move them around. Landscape had been simply a backdrop; artists began to make it a subject. Man's new position within nature rather than in front of it served both to diminish and to locate him. Altdorfer's St. George is a very modest figure who encounters his dragon in a huge, luxuriant forest that dwarfs them both; the sense of abundant natural presence surrounding and dominating the human presence is remarkable. Man is no longer "Master and Emperour of this Universe";[2] he must coexist with nature, perhaps not even on equal terms.

The analogy is useful to an attempt to understand what is accomplished by the spatial innovation in *A Midsummer Night's Dream.* A comparison of the wood scenes in *Titus* and *Two Gentlemen* with those in the *Dream* will yield differences comparable in effect to those between Renaissance and Mannerist painting. The woods in the earlier plays, like the backgrounds in the earlier pictures, have little interest in themselves. They are merely backdrops for the action and do not even require realistic expression. The woods of the *Dream,* on the other hand, described in detail and reinforced by embodiment in the fairies, are a powerfully felt presence in the play, an integral part of the action.

Bringing nature into the foreground naturally gave rise to a greater care in the depiction of detail. In art and literature, a limited naturalism was coming to prevail; artifice had not been abandoned, but it had begun to exist in a curious mixture with detailed fidelity to nature:

2. "Is it possible to imagine any thing so ridiculous, as this miserable and wreched creature, which is not so much as master of himself, exposed and subject to offences of all things, and yet dareth to call himselfe Master and Emperour of this Universe? In whose power it is not to know the least part of it, much lesse to command the same" (Montaigne, "Apologie," 2, 141).

If we study the art of the late Mannerists, we notice that in
spite of increasing involution and artificiality in the general
concept, there was a considerable increase in the study of
nature and in realism of details. We see this clearly in the
works of the landscape painters. . . . Scientific objectivity
grows in the same degree as irrational complexity of invention.[3]

The literary equivalent of the earlier use of detail in the pictorial arts is surely the kind of landscape in which we encounter
Tamora:

> My lovely Aaron, wherefore look'st thou sad,
> When every thing doth make a gleeful boast?
> The birds chaunt melody on every bush;
> The snake lies rolled in the cheerful sun;
> The green leaves quiver with the cooling wind
> And make a checker'd shadow on the ground:
> Under their sweet shade, Aaron, let us sit,
> And whilst the babbling echo mocks the hounds,
> Replying shrilly to the well-tun'd horns,
> As if a double hunt were heard at once,
> Let us sit down and mark their yellowing noise.
>   (*Titus*, II.2.10–20)

Nature here is emblematic, a bird on every bush, evoked first as
contrast to Aaron's mood, then as background for a picture in
which Tamora and her lover occupy the center foreground like,
as she says a moment later, Dido and Aeneas in their cave. It
is instructive to compare it to Titania's great landscape:

> Therefore the winds, piping to us in vain,
> As in revenge, have suck'd up from the sea
> Contagious fogs; which falling in the land

---

3. Benesch, *Art of the Renaissance*, p. 136.

Have every pelting river made so proud
That they have overborne their continents:
The ox hath therefore stretched his yoke in vain,
The ploughman lost his sweat, and the green corn
Hath rotted ere his youth attain'd a beard;
The fold stands empty in the drowned field,
And crows are fatted with the murrion flocks;
The nine men's morris is fill'd up with mud,
And the quaint mazes in the wanton green
For lack of tread are undistinguishable.

(II.1.88–100)

There is artifice in this picture too, personification and a distinct formality of presentation. But the difference is obvious.
The picture has at once greater scope and more exact detail.
Nature is depicted in large measure for her own sake. The
imagination ranges across the series of glimpses with an interest
unknown to the earlier outlook. And literal human presence is
optional; there may be a ploughman struggling behind his
oxen, but there may just as well be crows or an empty fold in
a drowned field. The earlier concept of nature has undergone
important transformation, and the increased interest in its details is coupled with a strong sense of its changeability. Tamora's
nature is relatively static; Titania's is mutable, Montaigne's new
reality, the "languishing and wavering dance" that surrounds
man and limits his understanding. F. P. Wilson writes:

> If, as some hold, the essential difference between baroque
> art and the art of the High Renaissance lies in the attempt
> to express and enhance elapsing moments of ever-changing
> Nature rather than the idea of Nature as a perennial reality,
> then Donne's poetry has a better claim to be called baroque
> than Spenser's, Webster's plays than Marlowe's, and Bacon's
> prose than Ascham's or Hooker's.[4]

4. F. P. Wilson, *Elizabethan and Jacobean* (Oxford, 1945), p. 26.

But the depiction of "ever-changing Nature," if we have looked closely at *A Midsummer Night's Dream,* is not so much a matter for post-Elizabethan literature as this comment suggests, particularly if we remind ourselves of the existence of Spenser's "Mutability Cantos," which fall so close to the writing of the *Dream.* The transitional character of Shakespeare's art or, for that matter, Spenser's had no need to wait upon the death of monarchs. The sense of an unstable and mysterious natural world which was to become a standard ambience in Shakespeare's work can be traced back to its beginnings in *The Comedy of Errors* and the early histories, and its development can be viewed in the interruptive ending of *Love's Labour's Lost* and the language with which Richard II accompanies his bitter downfall. It is the way in which this view of an abundant, indifferent, mutable nature is intimately bound up with style, characterization, and general dramatic effectiveness in *A Midsummer Night's Dream* that makes it such an excellent source for our understanding of Shakespeare's attitude toward nature and such a remarkable microcosm of at least one major phase of the cultural transition of its time.

Another distinctive feature of the *Dream* that seems to mirror a widespread change of sensibility in arts and learning (even, perhaps, to herald it) is the use of polarities held in balance, unresolved opposites. We cannot, of course, press this too far; the use of oppositions is always, to some degree, characteristic of the drama. Indeed, it can be argued that the art and psychology of the seventeenth century turned to the drama for inspiration and grew dramatic because, as Wylie Sypher has pointed out, *"the dramatic act can accommodate opposites as logic cannot."*[5] Nevertheless, it is possible to discern a difference between the use of polarities in, say, Marlowe and Lyly and in the *Dream,* a difference which lies in the area of our

5. Wylie Sypher, *Four Stages of Renaissance Style* (New York, 1955), p. 162.

reactions to them, our sense of their stability and truth. Here is one critic's version of the difference as he finds it in lyric poetry:

> The complexities of existence were more conscientiously, if not more conclusively, represented in the Baroque than in the Renaissance lyric. It might be shown that the "polarities," time and eternity, the physical and the spiritual, the microcosm and the macrocosm, produced tensions, not doctrinally resolved, which had gone unexploited in previous poetry; and that, in order to cope with their complexities and also with the intricacies of human relations, each polarity was expressed in such a way as to take its opposite into account.[6]

To a certain extent, of course, this is true of all poetry and all drama or at least of more periods than one. But when the tensions are "not doctrinally resolved" and when they tend to take their opposites into account, we have a genuine and important difference. In describing *A Midsummer Night's Dream* we can go even further, pointing out the extent to which traditional polarities—dreaming and waking, shadow and substance, imagination and reason, nature and art—are shown to have an instability which, in this case, gives rise to large, comic ironies.

A Midsummer Night's Dream, then, can be seen as a remarkable work of transition, one with affinities in at least two directions. Its tidiness of form, structural symmetry, and consistent comic tone all serve to link it to the art of the Renaissance. But its substance, rich and full of unresolved opposites, tinged with irony and skepticism about traditional values, brings it surprisingly close to the definitions of later styles. "Mannerism," says Sypher, "means experimental response, tentative commitment, learned but personal research, overcleverness in handling

6. Lowry Nelson, Jr., *Baroque Lyric Poetry* (New Haven, 1961), p. 14.

conventional forms and elements."[7] One thinks of Bottom and Titania strolling solemnly through the vast, moonlit forest: conventional elements cleverly, perhaps overcleverly, brought together. It is a strange, resonant moment, and if we have tended to ignore its strangeness and resonance, it is perhaps because our traditional means of categorization have obscured its unique relation to its age.

What of the *Dream's* relation to Shakespeare's own body of work? It is tempting, after such close study, to exaggerate its role as a watershed in Shakespeare's development as an artist. Certainly it can be shown to prefigure later works in important ways. In its use of the play within a play and of theatrical metaphor as expression of illusory reality, it looks forward to *Hamlet;* in its intense depiction of nature through listing and panoramas, it creates a basis for similar effects in *Lear;* and its invocation of a mysterious world shot through with magic, myth, and metamorphosis unmistakably reminds us of *The Tempest* and *The Winter's Tale.* An exploration of such resemblances might occupy us at some length.

At the same time, however, it must be admitted that the remarkable effects of the *Dream* are themselves prefigured in earlier plays by Shakespeare. So steady and continuous is his development as an artist that nothing really can be said to spring full-blown into the midst of his work; the scrupulous commentator can always find earlier uses in more rudimentary forms.

If claims of original formulation are dangerous, then, we can still stress the importance of the *Dream* as a stage in Shakespeare's development. His view of nature may find its beginnings in, say, *The Comedy of Errors,* but we are hardly likely to draw from that play a coherent account of that view. The dream–shadow–theater cluster of images as expression of the appear-

7. Sypher, *Four Stages,* esp. pp. 140–62.

ance–reality theme may have precedents in *The Taming of the Shrew* and *Two Gentlemen of Verona,* but Bottom's dream, like Hamlet's play, Antony's legend, and Prospero's masque, has an informing power as dramatic metaphor and unifying symbol that Sly's dream and Julia's disguise seem to me to lack. It is the *extent* of Shakespeare's accomplishment that makes the *Dream* comparable to later works and distinguishable from earlier ones.

Indeed, our main emphasis ought to be not that the *Dream* paves the way for later masterpieces, but that it is such a striking accomplishment in its own right. The dramatist, after all, was not simply readying himself for the writing of *Henry IV* or *Hamlet* or *Lear*. He was dealing with the problem at hand. He wanted to free himself, as far as possible, from any constricting limitations imposed by the conventions of his theater and the tastes and demands of his audience, to set styles and fashions rather than follow them. He wanted an inclusive art with the widest possible appeal and as complete a wedding as possible of rhetorical means and dramatic effects, language and action. These were the difficulties he had faced in his earlier works. What I have tried to show is how much the *Dream* had to do with the solving of such problems and how distinctly it is marked by the artist's own sense of his achievement and its basis, a strong creative imagination and a clear understanding of the nature of illusion.

If we must talk of watersheds, then we would do well to consider every drama as a watershed, an end in itself, another attempt by an artist to transform the familiar and the particular into the widest possible universe of meaning. In every attempt to make a play, the great playwright

> finds his own ways to enlarge the content of his play, to deepen its significance, and to reach out beyond a given

pattern of character and event to a universe of thought and experience of which they are but a representative fragment.[8]

What finally makes *A Midsummer Night's Dream* so interesting is not its advance over earlier works or its relation to later ones, but its astonishing success at the task described above, its vivid life as a "representative fragment."

Finally, we must ask if the conclusions drawn by this study lead to any new insights about Shakespeare himself, the artist as revealed in his work. Any answer will be difficult. Overriding all our brave attempts to prove Shakespeare a Stoic or a "Christian Humanist," a passionate temperament or a cool intellectual, is the weight of testimony to his elusiveness. It is greater than the ordinary indirection or circumspection of the dramatist. Una Ellis-Fermor, comparing him to the Greek tragedians and Ibsen, has described the difference:

> Of the greatest dramatists of the world's literature, one alone, so far, has used the dramatic mode, and only the dramatic, for the revelation of his underlying thought. It is Shakespeare who baffles impertinent conjecture and unimaginative exegesis alike by affording us no re-expression of his implicit, dramatic utterance in terms of explicit commentary. The reading of life revealed by his plays cannot, as we have already noticed, be abstracted, for it is co-extensive with the plays themselves and can only be learnt by a lifetime spent in their world.[9]

Most critics would agree with this, although they might be led to argue about why it is true. Does it indicate that Shakespeare was less "committed" or that he had less interest in intellectual and moral issues than his fellow dramatists? Miss Ellis-Fermor,

8. Una Ellis-Fermor, *Shakespeare the Dramatist* (London, 1961), p. 13.
9. Ibid., p. 11.

it will be noted, assumes that there is "underlying thought," and I agree with her. We do not escape the difficulty by pretending that Shakespeare was a bland mirror of the world, without opinions of his own. But the absence of preaching and direct commentary in his plays does suggest that he regarded his art as an end in itself rather than a means to something else. It is not possible that Shakespeare's strongest single commitment was to his art, that the center of his belief was a preoccupation with the nature and method of that art, a preoccupation that led him to the unique position among great dramatists described above? What Miss Ellis-Fermor is saying, in one sense, is that Shakespeare's art, as he conceives it, takes precedence over all other commitments and beliefs. To this we might add that he was an actor, with an actor's sense of the intricate relations between seeming and being, reality and appearance, and of the possible superiority of seeming. Such a sensibility might well strengthen the reserve, the elusiveness, and at the same time weaken the demands of beliefs likely to rival the man's devotion to his art.

It seems strange that one should have to argue whether the world's greatest dramatist was deeply committed to his art. But the fact is that Shakespeare is often represented to us as a man with no great interest in the theater, sometimes even as one with a contempt for it. There are slighting references to actors, theaters, and even poetry in his plays, but these are either metaphors through which life itself is criticized or passages that are best understood as ironic. What is often called careless writing is better classified, we are learning, as failed experiment. And the argument that Shakespeare did not care enough about his plays to have them preserved is simply specious; the fact is that we have no idea whatever of his attitude on the matter.

But for Shakespeare's commitment to his art there is a good deal of evidence. The reiterated belief in its transforming and eternalizing powers expressed in his sonnets is not just a con-

ventional Elizabethan posture. Nor are the remarks we get from
Time the chorus in *The Winter's Tale* or Prospero's great
speeches about his magic in *The Tempest*. But we are concerned here with the evidence provided by the *Dream,* the
earliest dramatic handling of Shakespeare's vision of his art
and the fountainhead of its repeated treatment in later plays.
We shall draw no systematic aesthetic from the play for the
very reason given above: the dramatic utterance is not trans-
latable. But if we begin with the most direct and explicit (one
should say least indirect) moment in the play, Theseus' inadequate remarks about the value of the imagination, and regard
it as an expression of the play's central concern, then we can
see how the aesthetic preoccupation opens outward to take
in love and lunacy as well as poetry, to suggest, "following
darkness like a dream," radical insights into human psychology
and the nature of nature. The test of our success is the sense
of completeness and relevance that this approach affords us, and
that sense will vary from reader to reader. I am glad to have
evidence that I am not the only student of the play who has
found this viewpoint congenial. Elizabeth Sewell lists the
themes of the play: "nature, form, and 'method' itself, imagination in the working mind appearing here as myth, poetry, and
theater."[10] It is the view of imagination, I would add, that
determines the view of myth and form, if such a separation or
hierarchy is possible. R. W. Dent, in a recent article, demonstrates that the play is "a disarmingly unpretentious defense of
poetry by the greatest of England's poets."[11] Such a statement
may not seem startling until we realize its implications: if this
is Shakespeare's *ars poetica,* embodied in a perfected example
of the art, then it must be regarded as one of his most important
plays and a touchstone for the understanding and interpretation

10. Sewell, *The Orphic Voice,* p. 119.
11. R. W. Dent, "Imagination in *A Midsummer Night's Dream,"
Shakespeare Quarterly, 15* (Spring 1964), 129.

of others. Such is the claim this study has attempted to put forward.

Just how radical this claim is depends on how far one wishes to take it. Great effort has gone into the attempts to show how many conventions and attitudes Shakespeare shared with his audience, how adjusted and settled a man, in that sense, he was. Without such harmony of convictions, it is maintained, his art would have been impossible.[12] There is a good deal of common sense in this view, but it is damaging and dangerous, I think, if we allow it to control our view of Shakespeare, since it tends to put lids on his ideas or, to use a more appropriate figure, bottoms on his bottomless dreams. *A Midsummer Night's Dream* demonstrates that he was quite able to express conventional attitudes at the same time that he was exploring their opposites and transcending them. In the practice of his art he was, like Prospero, about as far from the ordinary as it is possible to be, and if he had no sense of that, he would have been remarkably oblivious indeed. If his art set him off from the conventional, it is only natural that he should have been aware of its power and that this awareness might to a large extent govern his outlook. He had no need to assert his uniqueness elsewhere in his life or by direct comment in his plays because he demonstrated it unfailingly every time he set pen to paper to create for the stage. Some such knowledge must have sustained him, suggesting gently, like the voice of Hippolyta, that the "story of the night," however fanciful, can be transformed and "transfigured" until it witnesses more than fancy's images,

> And grows to something of great constancy,
> But howsoever, strange and admirable.
>
> (V.1.26–27)

12. I have in mind, among other works, Alfred Harbage's *Shakespeare and the Rival Traditions* (New York, 1952).

List of Works Cited

Adams, Joseph Quincy, ed., *Chief Pre-Shakespearean Dramas,* Boston, Houghton Mifflin Co., 1924.

Alexander, Peter, *Shakespeare's Life and Art,* London, J. Nisbet, 1939.

Anonymous, *The Companion to the Play-House . . . ,* London, T. Becket and P. A. Dehondt, 1764.

Bacon, Sir Francis, *Advancement of Learning and Novum Organum,* ed. J. E. Creighton, London, Colonial Press, 1900.

Baldwin, Charles Sears, *Renaissance Literary Theory and Practice,* New York, Columbia University Press, 1939.

Baldwin, T. W., *The Literary Genetics of Shakespeare's Plays,* Urbana, University of Illinois Press, 1959.

Barber, C. L., *Shakespeare's Festive Comedy,* Princeton, Princeton University Press, 1959.

Benesch, Otto, *The Art of the Renaissance in Northern Europe,* Cambridge, Harvard University Press, 1945.

Bethell, S. L., *Shakespeare and the Popular Dramatic Tradition,* Durham, N.C., Duke University Press, 1944.

Bevington, David M., *From Mankind to Marlowe,* Cambridge, Harvard University Press, 1962.

Bradbrook, M. E., *The Growth and Structure of Elizabethan Comedy,* London, Chatto and Windus, 1955.

Brower, Reuben A., *The Fields of Light,* New York, Oxford University Press, 1951.

Bullough, Geoffrey, *Narrative and Dramatic Sources of Shakespeare* (6 vols. London, Routledge and Paul, 1957), *I.*

Bundy, Murray W., "Shakespeare and Elizabethan Psychology," *JEGP, 22,* October 1925.

Burton, Robert, *The Anatomy of Melancholy,* Philadelphia, J. B. Lippincott, 1869.

Campion, Thomas, *Works,* ed. Percival Vivian, Oxford, Clarendon Press, 1909.

Chambers, E. K., *The Elizabethan Stage,* 4 vols. Oxford, Clarendon Press, 1923.

————, *William Shakespeare,* 2 vols. Oxford, Clarendon Press, 1930.

Chaucer, Geoffrey, *Works,* ed. F. N. Robinson, Boston, Houghton Mifflin Co., 1957.

Clemen, Wolfgang, *Shakespeare's Bilder,* Bonn, P. Hanstein, 1936.

Coleridge, Samuel Taylor, *Coleridge's Shakespearean Criticism,* ed. T. M. Raysor, 2 vols. London, Constable and Co., 1930.

Craig, Hardin, *The Enchanted Glass,* New York, Oxford University Press, 1936.

————, *A New Look at Shakespeare's Quartos,* Stanford, Stanford University Press, 1961.

Davies, Sir John, *Works,* ed. A. B. Grosart, 3 vols. Blackburn, C. Tiplady, 1869–76.

de la Mare, Walter, *Pleasures and Speculations,* London, Faber and Faber, 1940.

Dent, R. W., "Imagination in *A Midsummer Night's Dream,*" *Shakespeare Quarterly, 15,* Spring 1964.

Doran, Madelaine, *Endeavors of Art,* Madison, University of Wisconsin Press, 1954.

Duckworth, George E., *The Nature of Roman Comedy,* Princeton, Princeton University Press, 1959.

Edwards, Richard, *Damon and Pythias,* in Hazlitt, W. Carew, ed., *Dodsley's Old English Plays* (15 vols. London, Reeves and Turner, 1874), 4.

Ellis-Fermor, Una, *Shakespeare the Dramatist,* London, Methuen, 1961.

Elyot, Sir Thomas, *The Boke Named the Governour,* ed. Foster Watson, London, J. M. Dent, 1907.

Evans, B. Ifor, *The Language of Shakespeare's Plays,* Bloomington, Indiana University Press, 1952.

Evans, Bertrand, *Shakespeare's Comedies,* Oxford, Clarendon Press, 1960.

Foakes, R. A., "The Comedy of Greene and Shakespeare," in *Early Shakespeare,* Stratford-upon-Avon Studies 3, New York, St. Martin's Press, 1961.

Frazer, J. G., *The Golden Bough,* abridged ed. London, Macmillan Co., 1954.

Frye, Northrop, "Characterization in Shakespearean Comedy," *Shakespeare Quarterly, 4,* 1955.

Gascoigne, George, "Certayne Notes of Instruction," *Elizabethan Critical Essays,* ed. C. G. Smith (2 vols. London, Oxford University Press, 1904), *1.*

Gosson, Stephen, *The School of Abuse,* London, Shakespeare Society Reprints, 1841.

Greene, Robert, *The Honourable History of Friar Bacon and Friar Bungay,* in Thorndike, Ashley, ed., *Minor Elizabethan Drama,* 2 vols. London, J. M. Dent, 1910.

———, *Greene's Groatsworth of Wit,* in C. M. Ingleby, ed., *Shakspere Allusion-Book,* London, New Shakespeare Society, 1909.

——— (attr.), *George A Greene, The Pinner of Wakefield,* in Adams, Joseph Quincy, ed., *Chief Pre-Shakespearean Dramas,* Boston, Houghton Mifflin Co., 1924.

Grossmann, F., *Bruegel,* 2 vols. London, Phaidon Press, 1955.

Halliwell-Phillips, J. O., *Illustrations of the Fairy Mythology of A Midsummer Night's Dream,* London, Shakespeare Society Publications, 1845.

———, *Memoranda on the Midsummer Night's Dream,* Brighton, Fleet and Bishop, 1879.

Harbage, Alfred, *Shakespeare and the Rival Traditions,* New York, Macmillan Co., 1952.

Hathaway, Baxter, *The Age of Criticism: The Late Renaissance in Italy,* Ithaca, Cornell University Press, 1962.

Haydn, Hiram, *The Counter-Renaissance,* New York, Charles Scribner's Sons, 1950.

Hazlitt, W. Carew, ed., *Brand's Popular Antiquities of Great Britain,* 3 vols. London, J. R. Smith, 1870.

Hieatt, A. Kent, *Short Time's Endless Monument,* New York, Columbia University Press, 1960.

Hooker, Richard, *Ecclesiastical Polity,* 2 vols. London, Oxford University Press, 1890.

Hull, Eleanor, *Folklore of the British Isles,* London, Methuen, 1928.

Hunter, G. K., *John Lyly,* Cambridge, Harvard University Press, 1962.

Johnson, Samuel, *Samuel Johnson on Shakespeare,* ed. W. K. Wimsatt, Jr., New York, 1960.

———, *Rambler,* 125 (1751), 1824 ed. London, Jones and Co.

Jonson, Ben, *Works,* eds. C. H. Herford and Percy Simpson, 11 vols. Oxford, Clarendon Press, 1947.

Kermode, Frank, "The Mature Comedies," in *Early Shakespeare,* Stratford-upon-Avon Studies 3, New York, St. Martin's Press, 1961.

Knight, G. Wilson, *The Wheel of Fire,* London, Oxford University Press, 1930.

————, *The Shakespearean Tempest,* London, Oxford University Press, 1932.

Kolbe, F. C., *Shakespeare's Way,* London, Sheed and Ward, 1930.

Latham, Minor White, *The Elizabethan Fairies,* New York, Columbia University Press, 1930.

Lewis, C. S., *The Discarded Image,* London, Cambridge University Press, 1964.

Lovejoy, Arthur O., and others, *A Documentary History of Primitivism and Related Ideas,* 2 vols. Baltimore, Johns Hopkins Press, 1935.

Lyly, John, *Works,* ed. R. Warwick Bond, 3 vols. Oxford, Clarendon Press, 1902.

Mack, Maynard, "The Jacobean Shakespeare: Some Observations on the Construction of the Tragedies," in *Jacobean Theatre,* Stratford-upon-Avon Studies 1, New York, St. Martin's Press, 1960.

Malebranche, M., *De la Recherche de la Vérité,* 4 vols. Paris, Chez les Libraires Associés, 1772.

Marston, John, *Plays,* ed. H. Harvey Wood, 3 vols. Edinburgh, Oliver and Boyd, 1934–39.

Merchant, W. Moelwyn, *"A Midsummer Night's Dream:* A Visual Re-creation," in *Early Shakespeare,* Stratford-upon-Avon Studies 3, New York, St. Martin's Press, 1961.

Mincoff, Marco, "Shakespeare and Lyly," *Shakespeare Survey* 14, London, Cambridge University Press, 1961.

Montaigne, M. de, *Florio's Montaigne,* Tudor Translations, 3 vols. London, D. Nutt, 1892–93.

Muir, Kenneth, *Shakespeare's Sources,* London, Methuen, 1957.

Nashe, Thomas, *Works,* ed. R. B. McKerrow, rev. Wilson, 5 vols. Oxford, B. Blackwell, 1958.

Nelson, Lowry, Jr., *Baroque Lyric Poetry,* New Haven, Yale University Press, 1961.

Nichols, John, ed., *The Progresses and Public Processions of Queen Elizabeth,* 3 vols. Edinburgh and Perth, John Nichols, 1823.

Olson, Paul A., *"A Midsummer Night's Dream* and the Meaning of Court Marriage," *ELH, 24,* June 1957.

Parker, Samuel, *A Free and Impartial Censure of the Platonick*

Philosophie, Oxford, 1666, in Bond, Donald F., "Distrust of Imagination in English Neo-Classicism," *Philological Quarterly,* *14,* October 1935.

Peele, George, *The Old Wives' Tale,* in C. F. Tucker Brooke and Nathaniel Burton Paradise, *The English Drama 1580–1642,* Boston, D. C. Heath, 1933.

Pepys, Samuel, *Diary,* ed. Henry B. Wheatley, 10 vols. London, G. Bell and Sons, 1928–35.

Pico della Mirandola, Gianfrancesco, *De Imaginatione,* ed. and trans. Harry Caplan, New Haven, Yale University Press, 1930.

Preston, Thomas, *Cambyses,* in Hazlitt, W. Carew, ed., *Dodsley's Old English Plays* (15 vols. London, Reeves and Turner, 1874), 4.

Price, Hereward T., "Mirror-Scenes in Shakespeare," *J. Q. Adams Memorial Studies,* Washington, D.C., Folger Shakespeare Library, 1948.

Puttenham, George, *The Arte of English Poesie,* eds. Gladys Doidge Willcock and Alice Walker, London, Cambridge University Press, 1936.

Robertson, J. M., *Montaigne and Shakespeare,* London, A. & C. Black, 1909.

Rollins, Hyder Edward, ed., *The Arbor of Amorous Devices,* Cambridge, Harvard University Press, 1936.

Rossiter, A. P., *English Drama From Early Times to the Elizabethans,* London, Hutchinson's University Library, 1950.

Scot, Reginald, *The Discoverie of Witchcraft,* London, John Rodker, 1930.

Sewell, Elizabeth, *The Orphic Voice: Poetry and Natural History,* New Haven, Yale University Press, 1960.

———, *The Human Metaphor,* Notre Dame, Ind., University of Notre Dame Press, 1964.

Sidgwick, Frank, *Sources and Analogues of A Midsummer Night's Dream,* London, Duffield, 1908.

Sidney, Sir Philip, "An Apologie for Poetrie," in *Elizabethan Critical Essays,* ed. C. G. Smith (2 vols. London, Oxford University Press, 1904), *1.*

Spenser, Edmund, *Works,* Cambridge Edition, ed. R. E. Neil Dodge, Boston, Houghton Mifflin Co., 1908.

Sprague, Arthur Colby, *Shakespeare and His Audience: A Study in the Technique of Exposition,* Cambridge, Harvard University Press, 1935.

Spurgeon, C. F., *Shakespeare's Imagery and What It Tells Us,* London, Cambridge University Press, 1936.

Stubbes, Phillip, *The Anatomy of Abuses,* ed. F. J. Furnivall, London, New Shakespeare Society, 1877.

Sypher, Wylie, *Four Stages of Renaissance Style,* New York, Anchor Books, 1955.

Van Doren, Mark, *Shakespeare,* New York, Henry Holt, 1939.

Vienna Kunsthistorisches Museum, *Katalog der Gemäldegalerie,* Part II, 1958.

Weinberg, Bernard, *A History of Literary Criticism in the Italian Renaissance,* 2 vols. Chicago, University of Chicago Press, 1961.

Welsford, Enid, *The Court Masque,* London, Cambridge University Press, 1927.

Whetstone, George, *Dedication* to *Promos and Cassandra,* in *Elizabethan Critical Essays,* ed. C. G. Smith (2 vols. London, Oxford University Press, 1904), *1*.

Wilenski, R. H., *Flemish Painters,* 2 vols. London, Faber and Faber, 1960.

Wilkinson, L. P., *Ovid Recalled,* London, Cambridge University Press, 1955.

Wilson, F. P., *Elizabethan and Jacobean,* Oxford, Clarendon Press, 1945.

Wilson, John Dover, *Shakespeare's Happy Comedies,* London, Faber and Faber, 1962.

Wind, Edgar, *Pagan Mysteries in the Renaissance,* London, Faber and Faber, 1948.

Wölfflin, Heinrich, *Principles of Art History,* London, G. Bell and Sons, 1932.

Index

(References to *Midsummer Night's Dream* are listed under the title of that play; references to other works by Shakespeare are found under Shakespeare.)